A VINEYARD IN
THE DORDOGNE

A VINEYARD IN THE DORDOGNE

HOW AN ENGLISH FAMILY
MADE THEIR DREAM OF WINE AND
SUNSHINE COME TRUE

JEREMY
JOSEPHS

metro

Published by Metro Publishing Ltd, 3 Bramber Court,
2 Bramber Road, London W14 9PB, England

First published in paperback in 2002

ISBN 1 84358 018 7

British Library Cataloguing-in-Publication Data: A catalogue record for this
book is available from the British Library.

Typeset by ENVY

Printed and bound in Great Britain by CPD Ltd

1 3 5 7 9 10 8 6 4 2

Papers used by Metro Publishing Ltd are natural, recyclable products made
from wood grown in sustainable forests. The manufacturing processes conform
to the environmental regulations of the country of origin.

Every attempt has been made to contact the relevant copyright-holders,
but some were unavailable. We would be grateful if the appropriate
people could contact us.

CONTENTS

FOREWORD

WHEN I FIRST approached Nick Ryman with the idea of writing his story, he told me in no uncertain terms where to go. Undeterred, I rang back. The second time he repeated his distinctly unwelcoming message even more vigorously. Despite that rather unpromising start, I eventually managed to persuade him of the seriousness of my purpose and after careful consideration he decided to give my project the green light. From the outset I emphasized that while my approach would be sympathetic, it would not be sycophantic. And to his credit, Nick agreed.

The Bacco family, Joseph, Agnès and François, whose

lives were intertwined with those of the Rymans for over twenty years, also cooperated with me fully, and I'll never forget the red-carpet treatment they gave me when I met them for the first time.

The writing of this book took over my own family's life, as I whizzed between Bordeaux, Bergerac, Paris and elsewhere. But in fact, each time I inflicted my offerings on my wife Clair, she proved to be a skilful editor in her own right, and much credit is due to her insights.

I must also extend a big thank you to all the Josephs, both in France and England, who helped me in the research and writing of *A Vineyard in the Dordogne*.

I would also like to express my gratitude to the following people, all of whom assisted in various ways. So, very many thanks indeed to Eric Allonge, Pat Atkinson, Agnès Bacco, Fabienne Bacco, François Bacco, Joseph Bacco, Anthony Barton, Richard Bartholemew, Malcolm Brinkworth, Ginette Cathala, Jonathan Cavender, Nick Cooper, Stephen Davis, Richard Dawes, Maryvonne Denée, Sue Donoghue, Carole Huber, Esme Johnstone, Sara Johnstone, Stan Kinns, Michèle Lattes, Jean-Louis Lesage, Jonathan Margolis, Charles Martin, Sylvia Miller, Gabrielle Mondié, Henry Mondié, Patrick Montfort, Emil Perauer, Anne Ryman, Dr Anne Ryman,

Camilla Ryman, Cicely Ryman, Corinne Ryman, Desmond Ryman, Hugh Ryman, Nick Ryman, Marie-Claude Sampson, Carole Sedler, Sian, Robert Smith, Marie-Pierre Tamagnon, Jean-Louis Trouillon, Murielle Valentini and Alan Whytock.

Jeremy Josephs

PRELUDE

IT HAD BEEN his dream for as long as he could remember. To live in France. To make excellent wine in a vineyard of his own. And to make his home in an elegant château. Was this not, Nick Ryman wondered, many an Englishman's dream?

From the very first moment he set eyes on it he had fallen in love with Château de la Jaubertie. 'That's exactly what I want,' he said to the delight of the local estate agent. 'I'll take it.' Not yet forty, he was in the fortunate position of being able to buy more or less what he wanted. All as a result of his own hard work, though, for he had spent the previous two decades transforming the family's small stationery business into a huge success and indeed a household name. Without hesitation he offered the full asking price of two million francs for the château.

The Sauvats, the wily owners, knew exactly how to handle their wealthy purchaser from overseas. For the next two years they were to blow hot and cold in respect of the sale, always managing to put up the price in the process. Nick Ryman had tried to free himself from the magical hold of Jaubertie. So too had his wife Anne. But to no avail, for in their search for an alternative they saw nothing to compare with it. Within two years the price had doubled. 'Offer four million then,' Nick told the agent.

On Saturday, 29 September 1973, Nick arrived at a notary's office in Saussignac, a small village just outside Bergerac in the Dordogne, ready to sign the *acte définitif*. It was with much relief that he put his name to that legal document, despite the fact that he was paying considerably over the odds for his *folie*. Then Monsieur Sauvat did likewise. But when it came to Madame's turn to append her signature, she appeared to hesitate for a while, as if overcome by the emotion of the occasion. Swiftly recovering her composure, she proceeded to give all those present a piece of her mind. I shall never sign for the sale of Château de la Jaubertie,' she announced. And with those words she picked up the notary's fountain pen and hurled it across the table. 'Never.'

THINKING
PINK

SHE WAS HOPING for a girl. Though when she thought about it more rationally Agnès Bacco knew very well that she really ought not to be expressing any particular preference. For by the early spring of 1963 she had been hospitalized for a little over a month in Bergerac, a picturesque Dordogne town and a centre of French gastronomy. There, just a stone's throw from the river that gives the region its name, she had been left with little choice other than to comply with her doctor's orders not to stray from bed so long as her bleeding showed no signs of abating. She might not have been able to read and write, but the rather squat, dark-haired nineteen-year-old hardly needed reminding that the chances of her pregnancy ever proceeding to term were slender indeed. Yet the fact that the odds seemed to be relentlessly stacking up against her did not deter Agnès Bacco in the least. For as long as she could recall she had dreamed of one day giving birth to a daughter. She therefore summoned up all her spirit, the only resource available to her, it seemed, and positively willed the baby within her womb to be well. A devout Catholic, she would while away the hours in hospital by repeatedly urging the good Lord to intervene on her behalf and bless her with the gift of a girl.

The following week Agnès's husband, Joseph, five years her senior, came to an informal accord with the temporal powers entrusted with his wife's care. Since no miscarriage appeared to have taken place Agnès would be allowed to return home provided she remained confined to bed for the duration of the pregnancy. That meant another seven months with her feet up – plus one injection per day for each of those thirty-odd weeks. A little sorrowfully, they returned to their village of St Germain-et-Mons, ten kilometres away, where Joseph earned his keep as a manual worker in the vineyards of Philippe Van der Molen, a Frenchman of Dutch ancestry.

Joseph wasted no time in adjusting his daily routine to meet the new challenges ahead. Before long he was as adept with a needle as any of the physicians or nurses who would call upon his wife, and soon learned to dispense with their services altogether. Each day, at approximately 6 p.m., after a hard day's labour in the vineyards but before the evening meal, Agnès would reveal her rear end for her husband's ministrations. With increasing confidence and expertise he would select a buttock and inject Agnès with the progesterone prescribed by the family doctor to help ward off the possibility of a miscarriage. For the time being this twin strategy of inaction and injection seemed to be successful, for Agnès's belly appeared to be growing bigger with every week that passed.

Wherever he went and whatever he did, Joseph preferred to proceed at a sprightly pace. He was often to be glimpsed at work, hurrying between one row of vines and the next as if he had an urgent appointment to keep. There could be no doubt that he did the work of at least two men, a fact which not unnaturally endeared him to his employer. Yet Joseph seldom paused to assess himself in such a way; he was simply doing what he enjoyed most of all – hard work out in the open. Short and stocky like his wife, he was endowed with an enormously powerful frame, while his face already bore deep lines carved out by years of physical labour in all weathers, giving him a much older appearance than that of a man only in his mid-twenties. A legacy of formative years spent in a hot climate, the sunshine still shone out from his dark-brown eyes.

Joseph's parents were among the 150,000 Italians who had chosen to settle in Libya after Italy's invasion shortly before the First World War. Forty years later, however, as the era of empire began to draw to a close, the Bacco family beat a hasty retreat to Italy, sensing that the days of their privileged lifestyle were likely to be limited. In that assessment they would in due course be vindicated. Returning to Italy, the country where their roots lay, they were startled to find an impoverished nation in decline, still reeling from the impact of defeat in war and, most worrying of all, with little to offer in the way of employment. They wasted no time in moving on again, this time to France. And it was in Bergerac, some years later, that Joseph Bacco had been introduced to Agnès by his brother, all of them part of the same close-knit Italian community who had come to France in search of a better life.

Working in the vineyards at St Germain-et-Mons was better than no work at all. Joseph Bacco was under no illusions about that. Nor did he harbour any grievance against Philippe Van der Molen, who proved to be a most charming man. Unlike other employers in the Bergerac area, he offered not only lodging but both free bread and wheat to his workers. Joseph's sole complaint was simple enough: a monthly salary of 220 francs was barely enough on which to survive. With his wife unable to add any income at all, he struggled to raise the money to buy the medication required during her troubled pregnancy. The regular purchase of progesterone meant that other items – essentials, not luxuries – had to be sacrificed. Only when reimbursed by the cumbersome machinery of the social security system could Joseph head off to the nearest store to buy food, the rice and pasta which had been beyond the young couple's means during the preceding weeks.

So France had indeed been able to offer employment, as well as the great natural beauty of the Dordogne valley, but the land of liberty, equality and fraternity had also become, for the Baccos at least, synonymous with an all-embracing poverty which time and time again threatened to overwhelm them. Joseph often wondered how he might be able to break out of this cycle of despair. Now, with the prospect of parenthood becoming ever more likely, he began to spend much time staring ahead into the uncertain tunnel of the future. But there was seldom any light to be seen.

On Christmas morning in 1963 Agnès went into labour, simultaneously sparking off sensations of excitement and fear. She was taken into Bergerac's main maternity hospital, not far from where she had spent a month at the beginning of her pregnancy, when the possibility of miscarrying had seemed perilously close. Twelve hours later, at precisely 9.30 p.m., a perfectly formed little boy, François Bacco, made his way into the world.

'I know that I had been hoping to have a girl,' Agnès recalls, 'but when he was born I was so relieved. It had been such a stressful pregnancy. Doing nothing had given me all the time in the world to worry. I had been very concerned that all of the medicines and injections might have affected my child in some way. It was so wonderful to hold him in my arms and see that he was perfect. So in the event I was happy to have had a boy. I just took one look at him and loved him right away.'

Joseph Bacco, too, was delighted to have a son. Unlike

his wife he had never boxed himself into a corner about the preferred sex of his child. But he had another reason to be feeling particularly pleased with himself when he visited Agnès the following day. He had heard that a much more attractive job might become available in the next few months and that he had as good a chance as any of securing it for himself. His hard work had evidently not gone unnoticed. The employment was as a manual worker in the vineyards of Château de la Jaubertie, situated in the commune of Colombier, nine kilometres to the south of Bergerac. The owner, Joseph explained, was a Monsieur Sauvat, who apparently enjoyed a reputation for strictness and had a habit of strutting around his estate kitted out in riding gear, including jodhpurs and leather boots. Clutching his tiny son firmly in his arms, Joseph manoeuvred himself so that he would be able to savour his wife's reaction as he prepared to play his trump card.

'And what's more,' he announced in a rather matter-of-fact tone, 'I've heard that the wages there are 450 francs a month.'

Mathematics might not have been Agnès's forte. And the experience of having given birth for the first time certainly meant that her mind was not as alert as might otherwise have been the case. But she realized straight away that what appeared to be on offer was over double her husband's salary.

'Nothing can be guaranteed,' Joseph continued, hastily sounding a note of caution.

But if things went according to plan and he secured the job at Château de la Jaubertie, then 1964 promised to be a most attractive new year indeed.

'François is our very special Christmas gift,' Agnès Bacco would explain to most of her visitors at the time. And as she did so she could not prevent herself from imagining that the job at Colombier was already Joseph's. Because she had made up her mind that little François Bacco would never want for anything in his life.

PUTTING PAPER-CLIPS FIRST

THE SCENE MUST have been similar in countless English households that cold Christmas morning. Each and every seasonal tradition appeared to have been faithfully adhered to. Darting around from one room to the next carefully putting the finishing decorative touches to her stylish suburban home overlooking the eighteenth green of Hertfordshire's Moor Park Golf Club and a lake designed by Capability Brown, Anne Ryman had gone out of her way to ensure the smooth running of the forthcoming festivities, with tree, tinsel, turkey and trimmings all attended to with impressive efficiency. It seemed that the only thing the attractive twenty-seven-year-old mother of two had been unable to organize in advance was for a thick blanket of snow to have fallen and settled during the night. For, despite the presence of a sharp chill in the air and an overnight frost, the Meteorological Office had correctly forecast that Christmas Day, 1966, was unlikely to witness even a single flake of snow.

But Anne had other reasons to be feeling particularly pleased with herself that morning: she was poised to produce a Christmas lunch which would make her the envy of family and friends alike. When she had popped an apple inside her huge 20lb turkey to both flavour and keep its meat moist, everything was ready. Then, sensing the enormous wave of excitement as her five-year-old son Hugh scrambled to unwrap his presents, while Corinne, fourteen months his junior, made short work of the paper covering hers, she paused to reflect on the silent miracle developing within her but over which she had not the slightest degree of control. Although delighted to have discovered that she had fallen pregnant for the third time, she was unaware that the sumptuous feast which she would shortly serve would also be providing nutrients and nourishment for a second little girl.

Anne Ryman had long been accustomed to the good life. Her parents, having excelled in the fiercely competitive world of heavy engineering in Scotland by specializing in the manufacture of cranes, had determined that their only child would have nothing but the best. They had headed south and settled in Gerrards Cross, Buckinghamshire, so that Anne's childhood and teenage years were as remote in character from the grease and grime of Glasgow's industrial heartland as anything could possibly be. Always cosseted and often indulged, she had enjoyed an endless round of classes in classical dance, horse riding and lacrosse. Although they possessed ample funds with which to finance their various projects, academic excellence had never been Isobel and Bennie Butters's overriding goal when it came to their daughter's upbringing. The priority was rather to ensure that she should emerge as an elegant and refined young lady. Everything revolved around that. And how better to achieve such an objective than to send Anne off at the age of seventeen to the select Swiss finishing school of Mont Fertile, on the banks of Lake Geneva, just outside Lausanne?

Not that being dispatched overseas so summarily had

given Anne any qualms at all. Indeed before long the
Butters's daughter, freed from the constraints of their
sometimes stifling control, was having the time of
her life.

Anne had had a passion for cooking for as long as she
could remember, so after Switzerland it seemed an
entirely natural progression to study at the Cordon Bleu
Cookery School in London's West End. The pretty
débutante was one of sixteen students to enrol at the
select school in Marylebone Lane that year, and one of
just eight to graduate the following year. The school's
aims were clear-cut: it set out to teach its students how
to cook first-class French food. With the English
economy expanding rapidly in the late 1950s, Anne
soon found herself recruited by the Glyn Mills Bank,
situated in the heart of the City of London, where she
was in turn issued with an equally unambiguous remit: to
prepare and present stylish meals for the bank's
directors, either when lunching alone or keen to impress
guests during more formal corporate entertaining.
Responsible for the running of the bank's large and fully
equipped kitchen, and with one butler and two washers-
up to assist her, Anne was in her element. Barely twenty,
she was apparently able to organize and cope with

anything. Asked by one of the directors to prepare dinner for sixty guests, she was not intimidated in the slightest. Having decided to serve lobster Newburg as the main course that evening, with its traditional wine and tomato sauce, she calmly ordered thirty lobsters and dealt with them herself when they arrived with their claws bound tightly in several large wooden crates which were stacked next to the kitchen's sparkling white-tiled walls.

It was in October 1959, while working in the City, that Anne received an unexpected invitation to a dinner-dance at Wentworth Golf Club, in Surrey. Her cousin, Mike Dawson, a golfer who enjoyed a considerable reputation as a Scottish international, asked her if she might like to attend. Since he was engaged to be married, Anne knew very well that she had not been invited to accompany him that evening. What she did not know, however, was that her cousin happened to be a close friend of another golfing enthusiast, a highly eligible twenty-eight-year-old bachelor by the name of Henry Nicholas Ryman – Nick to all his friends.

'I had imagined that there would be lots of people, that it was going to be a big party,' she recalls. 'But when we got there there was my cousin and his fiancée, together with another couple who were also engaged. The only one without a partner was Nick – and I soon realized that I was the partner for Nick. It was a blind date. I had no idea. It was all set up. I soon got over the shock of seeing us as a sixsome. Of course I had heard of the Ryman chain of shops. Nick and I chatted away and we got on very well. I was very naïve in those days though – much more interested in my horses than anything else.'

There were certainly no signs of any such reticence on the part of Nick Ryman. Quite the contrary. Here was a man who knew his mind.

'When I saw Anne for the first time she nearly knocked me out. I thought to myself, what an absolutely beautiful girl. She was tall, blonde and blue-eyed – and with a sparkling personality to match. For me it was undoubtedly love at first sight.'

Unlike Anne, who continued to live with her parents in Gerrards Cross, obliging her to commute to the City, Nick had had his own flat for some six years in Dean's Mews, a stone's throw from Oxford Circus, in the heart of the West End. From there he had led the life of a wealthy young man about town, always nicely turned out in a smart suit and impeccable white shirt, and with not much more on his mind than business and golf. Like the woman he was happy to have been seated next to at the dinner-dance, he had enjoyed a rather privileged upbringing. For his twenty-first birthday present in 1952 his parents had bought him a two-seater Jaguar XK 120 in which, with hood down, wire wheels spinning and twin exhaust roaring, he would regularly roar through the Hertfordshire countryside *en route* to work with his elder brother Desmond, both young City gents tenaciously hanging on to their bowlers, determined not to lose them in the wind. All in all it was not a bad life. And yet Nick had come to tire of it. Even golf appeared momentarily to have lost its allure. With his thirtieth birthday beckoning, he had for some time taken the view that the moment had come to think of settling down. Having returned Anne to her parents' home after their evening together, he harboured not the slightest doubt that she was the person he wanted to settle with. Three weeks later they were engaged.

Emotional and romantic by nature, Nick had popped the question at the Jolly Farmer pub in Chalfont St Peter, not far from Gerrards Cross. And as he did so he shared with Anne a dream which, for a number of years, he had chosen to keep to himself. 'One day,' he said, 'we will buy a vineyard and live in France.'

'This idea was most agreeable to me,' Anne Ryman explains. 'Because I had spent many holidays there, I could speak the language, and had always loved the food of France and the French way of life. But I still took Nick's words with a huge pinch of salt.'

She was right to do so. Because of more immediate concern was the fact that Anne's parents considered that matters matrimonial were proceeding altogether too hastily. While they were certainly in favour of the match, they nonetheless successfully pleaded the case for the passage of a modest period of time before the wedding ceremony should take place. But for Nick, who seemed to have been born with impatience in his genes, even eight months appeared an eternity. It was with some relief, therefore, that he finally heard the bells of St James's Church ring out loud in Gerrards Cross on 8 June 1960. It was a typical English country wedding, with the reception held at Anne's parents' home in a specially erected marquee. Of course, there was only one candidate for the role of best man: the mischievous matchmaker Mike Dawson.

Similarly, there was only one choice of venue for their

honeymoon. It had to be France. After spending one night in London, they loaded Nick's latest Jaguar, a new grey XK 150S, on to the ferry at Dover and embarked upon a gastronomic tour of France.

'I handed in my notice as soon as I got married,' says Anne. 'I had been very happy working at the bank, but that was the done thing in those days, at least in our circles. The wife didn't work – that was unheard of. You had children, you were a lady of leisure – and that was it.'

If the wife's responsibility was indeed to raise a family, Anne Ryman certainly did not allow the grass to grow under her feet. For precisely nine months and six days after she was wed she gave birth to her first child, a handsome, fair-haired boy named Hugh, whose mouth and nose, some said, appeared to be miniature replicas of his mother's.

Nick's love affair with France was nothing new. It could be traced back at least to 1946, when his father decided that they should attend the French Grand Prix at Reims.

'I don't know whether it was the garlic or the Gauloises, but I fell for the place right away,' Nick recalls. 'I got this waft as soon as we landed in Dunkirk and it was heaven. First of all we stopped at Soissons, and we then went on to have one excellent meal after another. I admired the attitudes in France. The racing drivers left Reims from the garages in their houses and headed off towards the racetrack, with all the gendarmes telling everybody to get out of the way. It was most exciting – the food, the wine, the cars. To my young mind that excitement equalled France – and I became determined to try to live some part of my life there.'

This was perhaps a rather grandiose ambition for a fifteen-year-old boy barely out of school. He had fared rather well in his School Certificate, true enough, but he hardly had an impressive list of qualifications to his name. Yet he was adamant that he would pursue his studies no further. But how would his father react to his unilateral declaration that the formal period of his education was now complete? Evidently with no great concern, for he simply said, 'Very well, if that's your decision then come into the warehouse on Monday.'

Having himself left school at the age of fourteen, 'Ginger Jack' Ryman knew that he was not in a strong position to argue the case for a prolongation of study. Besides, it had always been his hope that both his sons would one day follow in his footsteps by entering into the family stationery business. And now they had.

The
Stationery Trades' Journal

Is an independent organ and is ready to publish articles and correspondence from every point of view, in order that business questions may be fully ventilated. It must be understood, however, that the Editor does not accept responsibility for the opinions of any correspondents.

Annual Subscription 2/- to all parts of the World, Single copies 2d. Post free 3 stamps.

Telephone : Central 4476.   **DECEMBER, 1928.**   *Telegrams : Whitmaosh, London.*

In a West End Corner.

Messrs. H. J. Ryman's at Savile Place.

The stationery shop which is photographed above is interesting on many grounds. Tucked away, as it were, in a corner of the West-End, it illustrates the value of locality and position, for it seems to dominate the street from any stand-point.

It is one of the many branch businesses of H. J. Ryman, Ltd.; all of them planned and "dressed" on uniform lines, giving up-to-date efficiency without any frills. The broad bay windows of this shop must be envied by a good many commercial stationers.

The spot shown is Savile Place, Mill Street, which leads from Conduit Street to Savile Row. The building on the extreme left is of 17th century design and stands on ground which was formerly the gardens of Burlington House. The passage known as Savile Place was originally a pathway to St. George's Place. Mill Street was named after a mill on the site of Hanover Square, and the stream by which it stood accounts for the names of Mill, Brook and Conduit Streets.

Inside the passage on the right is a small mixed shop, which was formerly the Cartoon Shop which the Duke of Wellington often visited, and it was in it that this Ryman branch was started in 1904, removing to the present building in 1911. The alertness and completeness of modern merchandising are in no ways impaired, but receive a tone and atmosphere from the memories of past history which haunt the spot.

To all our readers we convey the old wish, "A Merry Christmas and a Happy New Year."

When this trade feature appeared, H. J. Ryman Ltd had already been in business for over thirty years.

A busy branch of H. J. Ryman Ltd in London's Mayfair before the Second World War, and one of the company's business cards.

It was his own father, H. J. Ryman, who had started the firm shortly before the turn of the century, in 1893, the publishers Collins having partly funded the venture. To begin with the business was based entirely in the

West End, the first shop being situated at the Oxford Street end of Great Portland Street. H.J. Ryman then proceeded to expand, opening branches in Victoria Street, Brompton Road and Albemarle Street, and before long shops appeared in Watford and Harrow, much further from the centre of town. By the time Nick and Desmond's grandfather died in 1931 he had succeeded in expanding the business into a highly profitable group of eleven retail outlets.

H. J. Ryman clearly had a knack of getting his own way. Not even the First World War could deter him. He considered that his son Jack had served England honourably enough, first in the Westminster Dragoons, where he had learned to ride, and then as a lieutenant in the machine-gun corps. Unlike many Jack had somehow managed to survive that carnage. To his surprise, when still stationed in France, he was suddenly called before his commanding officer and informed that no further military duties would be required of him. The hand of H. J. Ryman was not difficult to detect. He had taken it upon himself to write to both Lloyd George and bureaucrats alike that his son was now required to run the family business, and urgently at that. Against all the odds it had done the trick.

Jack's heart, however, never really lay in the world of paper, pens and pencils. He was more of a committee man and he saw to it that he was never short of a meeting to attend. For not only was he chairman of the local council at Chorleywood for thirteen consecutive years, but also managed to find time to chair the planning committee of Hertfordshire County Council, sit on the bench as a magistrate at Watford, act as a special commissioner for income tax in London and assist in the administration of the board of the local fire brigade. Little wonder, then, that the firm of H. J. Ryman Ltd saw virtually no expansion during his time at the helm. Not that it was easy to keep any business going, however well-established, during the Second World War. The head office was entirely burnt out during the Blitz and one shop front in the Strand was blown out so many times during almost continuous German bombing raids on London that Jack Ryman could think of no better solution than to replace the windows with hinged wooden boards, so that every time they were blasted they would simply flap back again. With paper strictly rationed and fountain pens difficult to come by, he showed much initiative by diversifying into the supply and sale of map flag pins, which family and friends would make and bag up by the hundred during the evenings at their homes in and around Chorleywood. His firm was soon supplying most of the map rooms both in Whitehall and elsewhere. Lloyd George would surely have been proud.

It was into this environment of blotting paper, ink, ledgers and staples of all shapes and sizes that Nick Ryman stepped, full of energy and enthusiasm, at the age of fifteen. In consideration of his labour in the firm's central warehouse in Clipstone Street he received a wage of £3 5s 6d per week. The young boy who had found school boring and who could hardly wait to step into the adult world of work suddenly found himself spending the greater part of his waking hours in a dingy, dusty and undeniably dirty warehouse in central London, selecting and packing up bulk stock in order to dispatch it to the firm's various branches around the capital and elsewhere. And as he did so, young Nick knew that he had never been happier in his life.

Born on 15 November 1931 in Chorleywood, Hertfordshire, Nick Ryman had spent his formative years on the family's four-and-a-half-acre estate named Sunshine House, once a home for blind babies before the building burnt to the ground. This was rather embarrassing for Nick's father, who happened to be in charge of the local fire brigade at the time. Amid the ashes and remains of Sunshine House, however, he had been able to detect a potential for development and promptly proceeded to purchase and reconstruct the entire site. But with the Rymans as its occupants the house did not always live up to its cheery name. For while Nick enjoyed an easy, relaxed relationship with his father, with whom as he grew up he shared an active interest in cars, things were altogether more strained with his mother.

This enduring tension was almost entirely attributable to the fact that she suffered acutely with rheumatoid arthritis – so much so that shortly before the outbreak of war in 1939, at the age of forty-one, she retired to bed, and seldom budged from it again. One attempt was made to correct by surgery a hip which had been troubling her, but since the operation was not particularly successful, she vowed that she would never again subject herself to such an ordeal. There was a wheelchair to hand, although it came to be used only sparingly since it always required an enormous amount of effort to get her in and out of it. The consequence of all this was that she remained bedridden until her death just a few months before her eightieth birthday.

'It therefore wasn't a normal, happy upbringing,' Nick remembers. 'You went to see mother every morning and evening. She wasn't a very happy or healthy lady. But I did inherit from her two things: a great sense of humour – in spite of her illness – and one hell of a temper.'

Outside of the home, though, there was much happiness to be found. Especially during the summer months when, together with Desmond and their sister Judith, Nick would set out to explore the sandy beaches of Dorset's Studland Bay. The family's network of prime commercial sites in central London could also occasionally confer the odd and unexpected advantage. One such was a ringside seat in the Whitehall branch, perfectly placed for the boss's five-year-old son to view the coronation of George VI in May 1937.

Thirteen years on it was Nick's turn to serve King and Country. By then his c.v. could at least refer to some work experience – almost three years in the Ryman's warehouse plus a short spell behind the counter in their Great Portland Street branch – but it still made far from impressive reading. Perhaps national service would give him a new sense of direction. In fact it took him off to

Egypt. And before he could think too deeply about the wisdom of having opted for Africa, he found himself whisked far away from the Clipstone Street warehouse to the remote location of El Kirsh, situated in the canal zone between Port Said and Suez. Thriving on the discipline meted out by the army, he soon rose in rank from private to second lieutenant, with some thirty people under his command. He enjoyed himself enormously, responding well to the military's brand of man management and insistence on punctuality – a training which would in due course serve him in good stead. In charge of a platoon of petrol tankers and with a staff car at his disposal, he would often venture away from his base camp and out into the desert on his own.

'One day I drove off of the beaten track and sat myself down on a sand dune. And I thought to myself, right, Ryman, what are you going to do for the rest of your life? As I sat there it was like looking into infinity. I remembered the wonderful taste and smell of the only wine I ever tasted as a child, Château d'Yquem, which my mother had introduced me to, and considered to be the finest sweet white wine in the world. I thought too of my travels around France with my father. And I decided there and then, whilst sitting on my private sand dune, as I call it now, that I would like to buy a small vineyard and to live at least some of my life in France. It was just a private thought that flashed through my mind. But I do remember how very powerful it was.'

And certainly easier to dwell upon than to achieve. However, having completed his national service and returned to the family stationery business, Nick suddenly found himself taken to one side by his father. Desmond had likewise been summoned for a quiet word.

'Right,' Jack began. 'It's now up to you two boys. Either you make it or you break it. But from now on I'm going to run my life looking after my county council, my urban district council and my fire brigade. I'll be much happier to leave you two to do whatever you think fit with the business.'

Nick and Desmond Ryman needed little reminding of the fact that they were the joint heirs apparent to the Ryman business. The deferential attitude of many staff members, some of whom had been in the firm's employ since the early days with H. J. Ryman, drove that message home almost daily. But aged only twenty and twenty-two respectively, neither Nick nor Desmond ever envisaged taking control so speedily. With his father's words still ringing in his ears, Nick's mind raced ahead. If he rose to the challenge then there was surely no reason why his dream should not lie firmly within his grasp. The formula was quite straightforward: make enough money first.

'I thought that I was extraordinarily lucky to have found myself in this position, with such a bright future ahead of me. But that meant that we had to work hard and make the business bigger and better. My brother and I had a little head office where we used to sit and plot and plan together. We were both ambitious. Not that we were terribly scientific about it, mind you – we just did it by the seat of our pants. Some of the old shops were looking a bit run-down. We knew that we had to modernize and get out of London if our plans were ever to come to fruition. It was Desmond, though, who always took the lead, and I followed. I always looked up to him, ever since I was a child. My contribution might have been to question if we could afford something; whether or not it was likely to prove profitable, and so on. But he was the driving force of the business without any question.'

'Absolute nonsense,' Desmond retorts. 'I don't know why he talks down his own role so much. We were joint managing directors. Nick was not the junior partner in any way, shape or form. I might have been the ideas man, but he had the key role of trying to keep the firm's finances together.'

Whatever their respective talents, it was clear that the brothers complemented one another. Wherever they went, whatever they did or decided, it was invariably together. Not that this constituted a dramatic departure from the past, for Nick and Desmond were always to be found playing together as children on Chorleywood Common, and spent long hours challenging each other to rounds of golf from the very moment each boy had learned how to swing a club. Twenty years on they remained inseparable, travelling into town on the same train, with Desmond getting on at Chorleywood, Nick at Moor Park, two stations nearer London, only to arrive at work and share the same office – and with hardly ever a cross word between them. Nor did the close of the working day signal an end to their intimate involvement in each other's lives, for there was a large circle of mutual golfing friends in England and family holidays were spent together at their shared seventeenth-century farmhouse just inland from S'Agaro on Spain's Costa Brava.

If there was indeed some special chemistry between

them, then it was soon put to good effect. The brothers opened up branches in the Midlands, Manchester and Scotland, often buying out existing businesses *en route*. By the late fifties they had manoeuvred themselves into a position whereby they were able to go public by taking over Dudley and Co, a small and struggling company listed on the London Stock Exchange. As their firm flourished, the programme of expansion continued apace. Within twenty years turnover increased sixty-four fold, from £250,000 to £16 million per annum. Over seventy new sites were opened, either through acquisitions or the establishment of new premises. With shops prominently positioned in high streets and shopping centres throughout the land, Ryman had become a household name.

For both brothers, good business became synonymous with good living. Nick had an endless succession of expensive cars – Ferraris, Bentleys and the like – and enjoyed an equally extravagant and luxurious lifestyle. He became an adept helicopter pilot and an active member of the Helicopter Club of Great Britain. So too did the energetic Anne, on one occasion winning much admiration by successfully landing a Hughes 300 helicopter on the aircraft carrier HMS *Eagle*. Each of their three children, privately educated at the best schools, was given a horse as they grew up: Tiger for Hugh, Champagne Perry for Corinne and Knocky for Camilla, born in the summer of 1967. For those looking in from the outside, the Rymans were unquestionably the epitome of success.

Despite his hankering after France, Nick's nature remained quintessentially English, especially his stiff upper lip. In the world of commerce his reluctance to express feelings of any kind had not hindered him in the slightest. On the contrary, his cool and distanced disposition had helped to make him a most effective negotiator. Not so, however, at home. He was a strict and non-communicative father with all of his children but most particularly with his son, and this apparent inability to demonstrate love or affection of any kind was already having a very negative impact on Hugh, Corinne and Camilla alike.

Not that Nick was sensitive to any such shortcomings in his behaviour. He had other matters on his mind. He could see that with the arrival of the first supermarkets in England the whole concept of retailing was changing. There appeared to be a general move away from traditional counter service, with everything stored away in drawers, and into the brave new world of self-selection. Sainsbury's had detected this and adapted accordingly. But for Ryman the key question was whether or not what was good for groceries was going to be good for stationery too. The brothers judged that on balance the answer was likely to be yes.

It was a high-risk strategy. But when the first Ryman self-service shop opened in New Bond Street there was an immediate and overwhelmingly positive response. It was deemed to be so avant-garde, in fact, that it prompted a leader article in *The Times*. One by one each shop was scheduled for its refit, and one by one the elegant, hand-made mahogany counters and fittings which had graced the first Ryman shops during the latter part of the reign of Queen Victoria were chopped up and burned. Whatever would the firm's founder have made of that?

Other ideas dating from the *ancien régime* were in due course dispensed with too; the Ryman brothers determined to brighten up their shops both inside and out. Filing cabinets were sprayed in bright yellows, reds and whites; box and lever arch files were now sold in blues, greens and pinks. The aim was to get away from the grey image of the past, and it proved a commercial triumph for the firm. And when, in 1967, Nick and Desmond acquired the Conran group, Terence Conran's input gave still more flair to their work, propelling the Rymans into the forefront of the ever-changing world of design.

Success was the watchword. But in the process of acquiring it Nick Ryman eventually came to realize that his thirst for further expansion had been entirely quenched. After the best part of twenty years building up the business, for him the adrenalin of challenge was no longer there. 'It all became too big,' he explains. 'There were so many administrative tasks to do, with analysts constantly coming down to work out how much profit we might have made on this day or that, and boardroom politicking all of the time. I felt that I had seen and done it all. In the end I really wasn't interested in going into the office any more, or talking about business at all. I just wanted to switch off and walk away.'

But how was he to free himself from his carefully crafted gilded cage? Always at his most incisive while soaking in the bath, as usual one morning Nick peeled off his clothes, stretched his slim six-foot frame, and prepared to relax mind and body alike. As he luxuriated in his bathtub he could see that there were few exit routes available to him. On the one hand he appeared to be entirely isolated – the only member of either Ryman family manifestly malcontent with his lot. Yet at the same time he was far from alone, for any decision he might wish to take was inextricably bound up with Desmond's intentions and vision of the future. There was clearly only one road to salvation, Nick concluded, pulling the plug from his bath, and that was for an outside purchaser suddenly to present himself, unexpected and unannounced, and offer a hugely inflated sum for the business which, by common consent, it would be sheer folly to refuse. Pure fantasy, of course, for, despite its success, there was no queue of prospective purchasers jostling with one another to acquire the stationery empire. Not that this meant that Nick's earlier dreams had been extinguished. He recalls his thoughts, as he contemplated the London weather in the autumn of 1968.

'Outside the sky is grey and bleak. A brief flash of Indian summer came and went a week or so ago. Today it can't make up its mind whether to rain or not and I can't make up my mind whether I need to turn the central heating on. "Why don't I go and live where it is warm?" I say to myself. "Why don't I go and live in the country, where life is quieter, where one can get away from sweating humanity? Why indeed don't I go and live in France? Surely life would be somehow more exotic, more colourful, more romantic? After all they take food and wine seriously, the French. And if I owned my own vineyard and grew a few vegetables, I'd be more or less self-sufficient before I began.'"

But so far the nearest Nick had ever got to making this vision become a reality was in building up his interest in wine. As the years went by he managed to establish a first-class collection. He was only too well aware though that a cellar in Moor Park, however well stocked, was a far cry from owning a vineyard in the Médoc or Provence.

His son Hugh, however, was more than happy with what his father had to offer. He would sometimes go down to the cellar merely to inhale the smell of the wooden cases and bottles of wine lying there gathering dust. And whenever his father organized a dinner or luncheon, it was only a matter of time before young Hugh would appear on the scene, politely asking for the cork and bottle, whose label he would carefully soak off and add to his considerable collection.

Sometimes, however, he would show less respect for

his father's liquid treasures, quietly slipping down to the cellar with his sister Corinne as his partner in crime. They knew exactly what they were heading for – the bottles of champagne. Their hearts pounding for fear of being caught, they would play out the scene again and again, allowing themselves just enough time to take one or two sips before effecting a hasty escape. But then drinking had never been the primary purpose of their clandestine visits. Their aim was altogether more straightforward: having given the bottle of champagne a most vigorous shaking, they would risk everything to see how far they could get its cork to fly through the air, driven on by the lure of records crying out to be broken.

Hugh's antics might not have given the impression of a shy and sensitive boy, singularly ill at ease with his father. Yet Hugh was always treated strictly and was often at the receiving end of Nick's sharp tongue. He came to hear one particular message so many times that it took on the air of an all too familiar refrain. 'What you need, my boy, is two years in the army.'

However, Hugh was not yet old enough for national service, which had, in any case, as his father knew full well, long since been abolished. Nick turned his attentions to boarding school, the time honoured means to a rigorous education favoured by the English middle classes. Not that Nick had himself been sent away from home as a child. Nor did he apparently consider it as an option for either of his daughters.

In some respects whether or not Nick was happy with what he had achieved was irrelevant, for his business now seemed to possess an unstoppable momentum of its own. Together the brothers had succeeded in transforming eleven retail units into no fewer than eighty-four. Thanks to their efforts and enterprise the firm had become the biggest commercial stationers in the land. Nick thus had every reason to remain confident that sooner or later these rather flattering figures would indeed arouse the interest of an outside buyer, setting him free at last.

It was Spain, though, not France, which for Nick had become synonymous with freedom, at least for a few weeks of the year. However, holidaying on the Costa Brava during the summer of 1969, Anne Ryman walked into the family's farmhouse kitchen one morning to prepare lunch, only to find her husband collapsed on the floor and unconscious. Nick had been in a rather spectacular waterskiing accident the previous day, but since he had managed to clamber back on to the speedboat, no one had given the incident any more thought. Anne, however, struggling to remain calm and in control, had immediately summoned assistance and driven Nick to the local clinic, from where a specialist was contacted.

The doctor wasted little time in deciding on the appropriate course of action. 'We are going to have to operate straight away,' he declared. 'It's imperative that we relieve the pressure on the brain.' And to drive his point home to Anne he sketched out a picture of her husband's head on an adjacent wall. He repeated that the problem had to be tackled by surgery as a matter of the utmost urgency.

'No, you're not going to do that. Absolutely not,' Anne Ryman replied.

'You do realize then, I hope,' the doctor continued, 'that you are taking your husband's life in your own hands.'

But Anne was adamant, refusing to be hurried into agreeing to an extremely delicate exploratory operation. On the contrary, she insisted, the most satisfactory solution was for her husband to be flown back to England. She hurried off to find a telephone in order to contact Desmond at the firm's headquarters in London.

Within an hour he had organized everything.

'I hired a jet from Luton airport and managed to get one of the leading brain specialists from St Thomas' Hospital to agree to come out on the plane with us, together with Nick's GP. When we got out there we met this little chap who said that he wanted to drill a hole in Nick's head in order to have a look. I told him that we weren't going to have anything like that happen in Spain.'

The local specialist had no intention of arguing with the growing Ryman entourage now at his hospital. He knew perfectly well what was going to happen if his advice was not acted upon within a matter of hours. And with that in mind, he sent for a priest, who, on being advised of Nick's critical condition, proceeded to administer the last rites.

For Nick, still in a coma as his plane climbed into the skies above Spain, the prognosis was very grim indeed. The fight was on for his life – not his dreams.

RED WINE IN HIS VEINS

IT WAS A spring to remember. At the Nanterre campus on the outskirts of Paris students had been protesting both about the shortcomings of the educational system and the practices of the international capitalist order, whose fundamental immorality seemed to be all too clearly illustrated by American policy in Vietnam. A combination of police brutality and ineptitude on the part of the University of Paris authorities ensured that a normally marginal group of Trotskyists, anarchists and Maoists were able to successfully stir up public discontent. During the afternoon of Friday, 10 May 1968 huge crowds began to assemble in the capital. The

CRS (Compagnie Républicaine de Sécurité), the French riot police, were likewise out in force. As they donned protective clothing and braced themselves for action, students in the Latin Quarter's fifth *arrondissement* were urgently erecting the first barricade in the rue Le Goff. The stand-off did not last long, with paving stones soon being ripped up and cars turned over as violent confrontations erupted and continued throughout the early part of the night.

By the following morning the world's most beautiful city more closely resembled a battleground. Three hundred and sixty-seven people had been wounded, four hundred and sixty students arrested for riotous behaviour and one hundred and eighty-eight cars either burnt out or otherwise destroyed. And that was but a foretaste of further trouble to come.

For the demonstrations rapidly spread into the provinces, with massive strikes and sit-ins around the country, involving over ten million workers. Not to be excluded, France's school students needed little encouragement before taking to the streets, listing a series of grievances and demanding urgent and immediate reforms. In the normally sleepy city of Béziers in the sunny southern region of Languedoc-

Roussillon, the state-run Lycée Henri IV was obliged to shut down early, thereby prolonging the already generous summer break, as its pupils occupied classrooms and distributed leaflets setting out their case.

There were not the slightest signs of any such stirrings or discontent, however, at the privately-funded and fee-paying Pensionnat de l'Immaculée Conception, only half a kilometre away. Popularly known as the PIC and created by a religious order at the beginning of the nineteenth century with a view to meeting the educational and religious requirements of the sons of the local bourgeoisie, the school occupied rather drab premises in the heart of the old town, dominated by the imposing fortified cathedral of St Nazaire, and overlooking the meandering River Orb. The pupils might well have read about the troubles in the press or watched television news reports, but every boy there had just one thing on his mind: to pass his *baccalauréat math-élém*, which meant a disproportionately heavy dose of physics, maths and French, and in so doing acquire the first and most important stamp on his passport to eventual success. With only a few weeks before the examinations were scheduled to begin, this diligent and devoted approach to study was particularly well exemplified by the twenty-year-old Henry Mondié. Having already repeated two school years in his academic career to date, including the key class of *terminal*, he had no intention of sitting for his 'bac' a third time. He would succeed in the summer exams of 1968 or never at all.

Maurice Mondié, Henry's father, might well have wished his own position was otherwise. But the fact was that he would have had much difficulty in offering practical assistance to his son should he happen once again not to score sufficiently high marks. For although he was a wine-grower by trade, with over twenty hectares of vineyards to his name, his estate had only ever been capable of generating one income, not two. And since his father was only forty-eight at the time, with retirement many years away, Henry knew perfectly well that he himself was unlikely to find a future in the vineyards of the Hérault. So too did his younger brother, Claude, who had no intention of toiling the land and was hoping to pursue a career in either banking or commerce.

The Mondiés were from the small village of Cruzy, twenty-five kilometres west of Béziers and not far from where the historic Canal du Midi cuts its way through the attractive reddish landscape on a small part of its long and winding journey from the Atlantic to the Mediterranean. With vineyards stretching out as far as the eye can see and producing for the most part the red *vin ordinaire* of the region, Cruzy fell within the Minervois and St Chinian *appellations* (vintages). Unlike the smart vineyards of the Médoc, where the vines often surround a show-piece château, the Mondié's estate consisted of fifteen different plots, in many cases separated from one another by nothing more than the *garrigue*, the rocky scrubland of the south of France.

Dark-haired and dark-eyed like the majority in the Midi, Henry had spent a very happy childhood close to the vineyards of Cruzy before being sent off to board in Béziers at the age of eleven. Cruzy, with its population of just 1,500, had been the centre of his world, with relatives, friends, school and catechism all within walking distance of his home. Although a small village, it boasted the magnificent church of Ste Eulalie, dating from the days of Pope Urban V, with a coquettish statue of the Virgin Mary inside, her hips inclining slightly to one side, and carved in the best traditions of the Italian Renaissance.

Proud of their Occitan past and always anxious to

respect both local and regional *fêtes*, the people of Cruzy, like those throughout the region, led a life that revolved around the production and consumption of wine. Each stage of the complex process of winemaking was the subject of intense scrutiny and heated debate — from the art of planting to the skills of bottling and storage. Whenever Maurice Mondié bumped into a neighbour or acquaintance in Cruzy's village square or Béziers' allées Paul Riquet, named after the engineer who constructed the epochal Canal du Midi, the conversation would inevitably turn to wine. And in the best traditions of village life every *viticulteur* seemed to know every other winegrower's business: what grape variety he was cultivating, where it was being grown, how many hectolitres he was likely to produce, precisely what stock was stored in his *cave* (cellar) at any one time and an informed opinion on the key issue of the most advantageous time to sell. In fact, by contrast with the many parts of France where talk of the joys of food is paramount, here the importance of wine surpassed even that sacred ritual.

Maurice Mondié might not have been able to guarantee a future to either of his sons. But that did not mean that life in the vineyards had not served him well.

His twenty hectares constituted a sizeable asset compared with other holdings in the area, and he was very much the *petit seigneur* of his domain. This brought undeniable advantages, such as working entirely at his own speed, and with more than the odd day off he would often stalk through the *garrigue* with his lightweight Plume rifle slung over his shoulder, in search of rabbit, partridge or hare. And since his wine often fetched healthy prices from the local *cave coopérative* (wine cooperative), to which he sold his entire produce *en vrac* (unbottled), thereby avoiding the costly processes of bottling and labelling, there was seldom any shortage of money for Maurice and his wife Juliette. For this reason it never once crossed his mind that he would in due course do anything other than enrol both of his sons at the Pensionnat de l'Immaculée Conception in Béziers, unquestionably the most select school in the area. For Maurice, tending to his vines was more of a way of life than a mere means of employment and, master of his own destiny as he was, it was a thoroughly pleasant way of life at that.

For his son Henry the greatest pleasure of growing up in such an environment was the simple joy of being out in the open. The undisputed highlight of his week was to be able to join his father, who, together with four or five of his workers, would have set off for the vineyards earlier during the morning to avoid the searing heat of the sun. These excursions would always take place on a Thursday, the day off from school in France during the fifties. Securing his balance on his red Motobécane bicycle, and drinking in the beauty of the landscape all around, he would pedal off to meet up with this small and informal party of workmen. But first things first. For Mondié junior always made sure that his arrival was timed to coincide with their hard-earned break for lunch. Then, settling himself among the adults in the tiny, ramshackle hut built on the site of the vineyard, he would look on as each worker in turn produced from a small container a delicious meal of sausages or stew. The men took turns to heat up their lunch over a camp-fire of old vines and with the smell of herbs and seasoning soon filling the air it was never long before the boy's mouth would begin to water in anticipation of the dish which his father would patiently prepare for him.

Henry Mondié's wholesome outdoor lifestyle was brought to an abrupt end, however, when the time finally came, as he always knew it would, for him to be sent off as a boarder to Béziers at the age of eleven. At first he found it difficult to adjust to the new and rather strict regime, where concern for the boys' moral well-being was accorded as much importance as their instruction in Latin and maths. But he at least had the opportunity of returning to Cruzy every weekend, only half an hour's drive away, when he would often accompany his father on an impromptu tour of inspection of his scattered *parcelles* of land. In addition, there was also the *vendanges* (wine harvest) to look forward to, which invariably took place in September and thus overlapped with his return to school. Aware of the importance of wine-growing to the livelihoods of almost everybody in the area, the ecclesiastical authorities responsible for the running of the school would issue a series of special derogations, allowing wine-growers' sons to remain at home for the duration of the harvest. During these few frenetic weeks the impression was given in and around Béziers, as in countless other wine-producing regions of France, that virtually every able-bodied person was hard at work in the vineyards, having heeded the urgent summons to assist.

Not that it was particularly glamorous work. At the age of twelve and thirteen Henry would find himself working alongside women whose job it was to cut the grapes from the vines with a strong pair of secateurs, as together they methodically worked their way from one row of vines to the next. But as soon as his body began to develop his father saw to it that he was given more physically exerting work, carrying large wicker baskets laden with ripe red grapes, towards a central collection point.

But cutting and carrying was not the role which Henry had in mind for himself. For as long as he could remember there was only one job which he aspired to or deemed to be sufficiently exciting and worthwhile — driving his father's red Pony tractor. When, at fourteen, he was finally given permission to take the wheel for the first time, it was as if a magnificent moment of liberation had come. Shuttling back and forth between the various vineyards and then heading off again towards the *chais*, the overground cellars where the grapes would begin their miraculous metamorphosis into wine, he bubbled over with enthusiasm and joy. And it was then that he began to wonder if a life in the vineyards might not represent the best pathway for a future.

The work was particularly hard throughout the wine-harvesting season, yet the atmosphere was one of an almost continuous *fête*. Of the twenty or so people working together, sharing in the common cause of stripping the vines of their fruit, the majority were Spanish, seasonal workers who had travelled up from the border, only a couple of hundred kilometres away. They would arrive at the beginning of September with two cases, one full of clothes, the other crammed to bursting point with Spanish food, which they evidently could not bear to be without and which always included spicy sausages and tinned sardines. The working day would begin at approximately 7 a.m. with a ninety-minute stint of picking and collecting before stopping for the *casse-croute du matin*, the mid-morning snack consisting of *pain de campagne*, charcuterie, cheese and ham, with a glass or two of wine to wash it all down. Then it was another few hours' labour before a still more filling lunch. And so on throughout the day until late in the afternoon. But since the same people, a mixture of Spaniards and village folk, would return year after year for the *vendanges*, strong friendships were forged, with more than the occasional romantic encounter. The same people would then meet up again during the evening, and basking in the sunshine which still remained, they would eat and sing and drink and dance their way into the early hours. And then the partying would abruptly come to an end for Henry, for, with hardly a grape left in sight, he knew that the time had come for him to return to the disciplined dormitory life of his boarding school in Béziers.

Every now and then, though, the Mondiés would themselves pack their bags and travel to Spain and visit the erstwhile *vendangeurs* in their new incarnations. There the patrons from France were received in a manner befitting royalty on an official engagement abroad, with magnificent paellas being served, the saffron-yellow rice always garnished with the most extravagant seafoods. It was a warm and friendly time when patrons and pickers alike would in turn relive the triumphs and disasters of that year's harvest.

It was as well for Henry that there was another passion in his life. He had been encouraged by his parents to join the scout movement at an early age, and the Baden-Powell philosophy of the teaching of practical skills combined with a healthy approach to outdoor living and adventure soon struck a chord in the boy. Before long he had fallen under the influence of his leader, Gilles d'Andoque, a man who impressed upon him the importance of assisting the underprivileged in particular and of doing good deeds in general. It all seemed to accord with everything Henry had learned both from his parents and during catechism in church. When the scout leader mentioned the possibility of assisting in the restoration of a rather run-down church in the area, as part of a long-term project for the group, the first and most positive voice in favour was young Henry's. In fact it was with more than a tinge of regret, even though he was by now twenty, that Henry realized that the time had come for him to leave his scouting career behind and move on.

In any case the *baccalauréat* (final school exams) now beckoned. And there were audible sighs of relief in the Mondié household, from parents and pupil alike, when, in the second week of July 1968, the news came through that this time Henry had been successful. At once the best bottle of champagne was brought out to celebrate the long-awaited occasion. Within a couple of days Henry was pondering his next move. He was tempted to study the new subject of computer science, having heard that the Institut Universitaire de Technologie de Montpellier, situated in the handsome capital of the *département* of the Hérault, offered an exciting and well-structured course. But anxious not to stray too far from all that was familiar to him, he was equally tempted to study oenology, which offered the possibility of his emerging with the prestigious status of qualified wine-maker. Encouraged by his school to set his sights high, he applied to the École Nationale Supérieure d'Agronomie (ENSA), also based in Montpellier and unquestionably the finest school of its kind in France. Hardly surprising, therefore, that when the selection board offered Henry a place he gratefully accepted it without hesitation.

Although hardly a hotbed of radicalism at the time, Montpellier's ENSA had been affected by the student uprisings during the course of recent months, in common with most other academic institutions. While there had been none of the violence that had characterized the demonstrations in Paris, classes there had been suspended for one month, as lecture theatre blocks were occupied and students voiced demands for a review of the school's approach to teaching. Because the ENSA came under the auspices of the Ministry of Agriculture in Paris, officials from the school hurried north to the capital to see which points, if any, they might be able to concede. Anxious to practise the politics of pragmatism, they had a number of reforms approved and rushed through by special decree, instantly making the school more democratic and meeting many of the students' demands.

By the time Henry first set foot in the school's imposing premises in the Place Pierre Viala, the wave of protest had passed and the administration had every reason to feel confident that the new term would get underway in an atmosphere of normality. Not that Henry had the slightest intention of reading the small print relating to the changes which had recently been introduced. His outlook was easy enough to understand: having spent eight years as a boarder in Béziers, where the concept of democracy was noticeable only by its absence, he felt that any kind of regime which the ENSA might have to offer was bound to be a dramatic improvement. Anyway he had come to Montpellier to study, not play politics, and he soon applied himself to the school's first-year programme of physics and chemistry, essential prerequisites for the detailed study of wine.

Student politics might not have been much to Henry's liking; but there were nonetheless other distractions lurking not far away. For the first lesson which he learned in Montpellier was one which did not feature on the school's syllabus at all — that the city student's life was very agreeable indeed. Then he made another major discovery that distinguished his present programme from the anguished days of Béziers and the *bac* — that once a student had been admitted to the ENSA, then, provided he worked reasonably hard, the chances were that he would in due course acquire the school's coveted diploma. By the time he returned to Cruzy for the Christmas holiday he had succeeded in making many new friends, having enjoyed a most hectic social life, attending parties in student flats and elsewhere several times a week — another far cry from his school-days. Now, instead of viewing the end of the holidays with a growing sense of unease, he could hardly wait for the new term to begin. Nor was it too taxing a task for Juliette and Maurice Mondié to detect the reason for Henry's uncharacteristic impatience. It was abundantly clear that their son had been applying himself with considerable energy not just to the subject of wine but to the study of women too.

The ENSA course did not disappoint Henry. Striking an excellent balance between theory and practical work, it required students to go off around the country for periods of work-experience training, and to make additional excursions to vineyards in various regions of

France. Every aspect of wine-making, it seemed, was covered, Henry selecting a special option on the economics of rural areas. He would never have dared say so in public, but the truth was that to himself he would periodically praise his own good judgement for having selected the stimulating subject of oenology.

As for the old university city of Montpellier, where sand, sea, sunshine and snow are never far away, it continued to provide the setting for the most magical years of his life. The place was teeming with students of all kinds, many of them drawn towards the famous medical faculty founded at the beginning of the thirteenth century, and Henry counted a couple of medical students as among his closest friends. One aspiring young doctor, having completed his internship in Narbonne, had taken it upon himself to invite both the student nurses and their teachers back to Montpellier for a *surboum* — a huge gathering of what appeared to be a significant percentage of the future doctors and nurses of France. It was at that party that Henry set his eyes for the first time on a pretty teacher of nursing, Gabrielle Montez, from the Lot et Garonne region, who had found work at the nurses' training college in Narbonne. Within two years they would be wed.

On completing the four-year course at the ENSA, Henry, though delighted to graduate, at the same time instantly regretted the passing of his carefree student days. And at twenty-four he did not need his parents to inform him that it was high time he found a job. Yet his prospects of finding suitable employment were not at all promising. But instead of bemoaning the fact, he decided to travel to Mexico to visit and work with his father's brother, Georges Mondié, who had a property and vineyards in that faraway land. At the same time he combined the trip with an extended honeymoon with his wife Gabrielle, whose job in Narbonne was to be held open for her. Three months in Mexico seemed to promise both an ideal transition from the years of study and an introduction to the world of work. But since the job was only a temporary assignment, it was not long before the newly qualified young oenologist began to wonder what the future might hold.

It was while tending his uncle's vineyards in Mexico that Henry received a letter from France. An old friend, Jean Abeille, had decided to get in touch. It was clear from the rather breathless tone of his letter that when he was not working, the greater part of his time and energy went into managing the association of former ENSA students. Aware that Henry had still to secure long-term employment, he wondered if he might be able to assist. And he proceeded to describe a particular client of his who had recently acquired a vineyard and who was anxious to recruit a qualified wine-maker. Not only that, Jean explained, but the person concerned was adamant that any candidate should be a graduate of the Montpellier school of oenology. That evening Henry sat down and set about drafting his reply.

AN ENGLISHMAN'S HOME

4

IT WAS TRULY a pitiful sight. Sprawled out on the floor of an aeroplane, surrounded by his wife and three young children and still struggling to regain consciousness, Nick Ryman was returning to England in a manner which none of the family could have envisaged. Just as well then that Reg Kelly, the British brain surgeon accompanying them, soon came up trumps. Throughout the two-and-a-half-hour flight from Spain to Luton he sat with his feet pointing forwards in a V-shape, with his patient's head wedged firmly in between them. At the same time he managed to balance two-year-old Camilla Ryman on his lap and read to her so animatedly that the roar of the jet's engines was periodically punctured only by her high-pitched pleas of 'again' when, from time to time, his energy appeared to falter. As for Desmond, responsible for organizing the entire trip, he suddenly found himself stranded that Sunday on the Costa Brava, since, having swallowed up the large returning Ryman entourage, the privately owned eight-seater De Haviland H.S. 125 plane could no longer accommodate his towering six-foot-two frame. He could hardly believe that just a few hours earlier he had been minding his own business quietly mowing the lawn of his immaculately kept garden in Chorleywood.

Reg Kelly, once back at his base at St Thomas' Hospital, facing the Houses of Parliament across the Thames, returned to his more conventional role. Among the series of tests he carried out on his comatose patient was a lumbar puncture, the insertion of a needle between the vertebrae at the base of the spine in order to tap cerebrospinal fluid. When the surgeon saw that there was not the slightest sign of any bleeding along the length of the spinal cord he inclined towards a diagnosis of contrecoup, an injury in which one side of the brain is bruised as a result of a blow to the opposite side. In effect, Nick's brain had shifted slightly inside the skull, such was the force of the fall. Unlike his Spanish counterpart, who had earlier sought to impress upon Anne the importance of an urgent operation designed to relieve the pressure on her husband's brain, Reg Kelly decided to do nothing but allow the passage of a relatively short period of time in which, he predicted, the bruising would probably subside. Three days later, not only had Nick emerged from his coma, but he was also well on the road to recovery, although there did appear to be a marked loss of control over his right hand. To Nick's loved ones anxiously looking on, however, there were more worrying changes than that physical disability.

'After the water-skiing accident there was a definite shift in Nick's personality,' Desmond Ryman explains. 'Everyone noticed it. He became more difficult than before. You can't remain in a coma for three days and then just carry on as if nothing at all has happened, because the truth is that certain brain cells die. Up until then Nick had always been very cautious, working everything out meticulously – and that seemed to go. Plus let's say that his short fuse became even shorter.'

In addition Nick had become more determined than ever to walk away from the vast Ryman business empire, despite the impressive list of material advantages which it continued to confer upon him and his family. And yet another two years were to elapse before he felt that the moment had finally come for him to think of breaking free. He did not know it at the time, of course, but freedom was about to be bestowed upon him courtesy of Burton, the Leeds-based men's 'tailors of repute'.

Aware of the success of the Ryman stores and anxious to diversify their business interests, Ladislas Rice, the Harvard-educated joint chief executive of Montagu Burton Ltd, invited the two brothers to lunch at St George's Hotel, a stone's throw from the headquarters of the BBC, in the West End. It was an approach which came as a complete surprise. Equally unexpected was that the prospective buyers wanted nothing to do with Habitat, then part of the Rymans' interests, and that their eyes were fixed firmly and exclusively on the stationery business. A series of more detailed talks followed, the key meeting taking place at Rice's club in St James's. The joint chief executive announced that they were prepared to pay £8.8 million.

'I couldn't believe the size of this sum,' Nick admits. 'Nor could Desmond. We looked at one another and realized right away that this was overvaluing us considerably – it was ridiculously high. As such it would have been absolute madness to refuse. Before all of this happened we had bought Conran, the Habitat group, which was then still in its embryonic stages. Terence was quite impossible to work with, and in any case we knew that Terence wanted to take the Habitat group back.'

It was a meeting to remember. Everything seemed to fit into place. As the directors of Ryman and Burton retreated to their respective camps, Desmond turned to his brother to discuss the prospect of a deal. But when it came to it neither man had much to say. Desmond simply ventured, 'Why don't we?', to which Nick readily replied, 'By God, let's do it.'

For a while it appeared as if the Burton deal might fall through. The company's executives and accountants began to introduce new conditions, pressing for a detailed inspection of the Rymans' books. Perhaps they were having second thoughts. But Desmond stood firm, insisting that the intending buyers knew perfectly well what the business consisted of and that they could therefore take it or leave it. If this approach was designed to bring matters to a head it succeeded, for they took it without further ado. And in doing so they saw to it that each brother, instead of enjoying a healthy salary and owning shares in the business, suddenly found himself in possession of a seven-figure fortune.

To Nick this most unexpected of deals tasted particularly sweet. For now his new life could indeed begin – and he still had a few months in hand before hitting forty. Once the deal was signed and sealed, Nick was soon knocking on the door of the joint chief executive of the newly enlarged Burton group. He had an urgent message to convey.

'I would very much like to retire or change direction immediately,' he announced.

'By all means,' Ladislas Rice replied. 'You are on unpaid leave immediately. Tell me, though, what are you going to do?' Nick knew precisely what he was going to do. It was what had been at the back of his mind for as long as he could remember.

'I am going to go and buy myself a vineyard,' he answered immediately.

'Once the money was in the bank,' Nick explains, 'the feeling was one of absolute relief. I was so happy to be out of business – and happy at the prospect of leaving England, at least for some time of the year. I'm an old-fashioned traditionalist really and it very much saddened me to be witnessing England in a state of decline. Things seemed to be evolving rather differently in France, where I could see that the railway stations were painted up, the roads were being modernized, the little villages all had their new *salles des fêtes* [community centres], the hospitals were second to none, the schools excellent – and so on. I suppose you could call me a rat for wanting to leave the sinking ship. That's not the truth of the matter, though. It was just that I wanted to have a go at making excellent wine and fulfil a dream.'

Having waited the best part of twenty years for this moment of liberation, Nick began to act with the vim and vigour which had deserted him for so long. No more dark clouds now. Suddenly there was no time to lose. Within a week of the Burton deal going through, he was speeding off towards France in a maroon Jaguar 4.2 saloon, impatient to begin the search for the vineyard which he had dreamed of for so long. Ten days later he was back in England, having looked at the five major wine-growing areas of France – the Loire, Alsace, Burgundy, Bordeaux and the Rhône – and was ready to report back to his wife. He soon discovered though that a significant part of his trip had been in vain.

'Right,' Anne said, 'forget everything north of the Loire – I want somewhere where the sun shines.'

So this time they travelled to France together, except in an even faster car, a dark-blue Ferrari 365 2 + 2 with red leather upholstery. They headed towards Bordeaux, although they did not remain there for very long. 'I've never been that keen on the Médoc,' Nick explains. 'Its wines are first-class but to me it's a very flat, sad part of France.'

Next stop: the Bouches-du-Rhône. But there they found the mistral blowing in full force and the July sunshine too hot to endure. As for Provence, it was arid, dusty and hotter still. 'You got to the top of the hills and you couldn't see the area because it was shimmering in the heat. My wife said that I couldn't possibly work in such conditions and I agreed.'

Three of the main wine-growing regions had been deleted from their list. Familiar with France from her many holidays there during her childhood and teens, Anne suggested that they drive towards the Dordogne valley, long a favourite haunt of the English, and spend the weekend relaxing there. Heading north-west in their stylish sports car, they approached the area by way of Cahors, the capital of the Lot et Garonne *département* and famed for its heavy, almost black wines. Nick enquired in the town if there were any vineyards for sale. There were not.

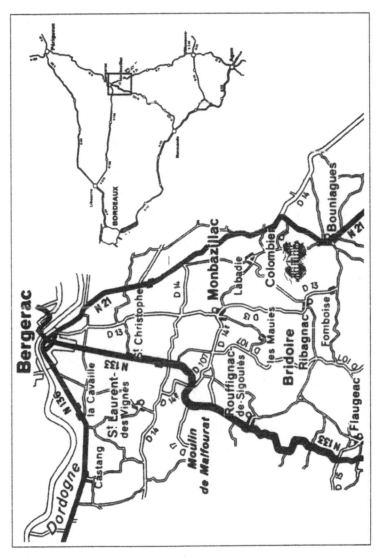

The village of Colombier, in which stands Château de la Jaubertie, is some nine kilometres south of Bergerac.

Undeterred, the Rymans pressed on, stopping overnight at Le Bugue, in the heart of the Dordogne's cave country, and not so far from the Grotte de Lascaux, containing one of the most outstanding displays of prehistoric art ever discovered, its steep galleries all magnificently decorated with engraved, drawn and painted animals. And it was in the Dordogne valley, rather reminiscent of England with its luscious rolling green countryside, that the couple immediately felt at ease. Confident that they had at last found a geography and climate to match their requirements, they again sought out the name and address of an estate agent who dealt in vineyards. It was the restaurateur at whose establishment they had stayed in Le Bugue who suggested that they make contact with a Monsieur René Chassagne. But all the agent could offer was a most unsatisfactory site. Why on earth was it so difficult, the Rymans wondered, to find the property of their dreams?

'I told him that I wanted a vineyard with an old house,' says Nick, 'on top of a hill preferably, entirely surrounded by its own vines, and ideally with round towers and square towers and turrets. Chassagne looked at me as if I was a bit demented and told me that they didn't have such things in the Dordogne.'

Even the Périgord, it seemed, famed for its countless châteaux, could not provide what it was the Rymans were looking for. But reluctant to relinquish his well-to-do English clients quite so easily, Chassagne spoke of an important property, Château de la Jaubertie, situated in the tiny village of Colombier, to the south of Bergerac, which had only recently come on to the market. And he produced a photograph of Jaubertie for the Rymans to inspect. It hardly seemed suitable at all.

'Look,' the estate agent insisted, 'it's only a short drive away. Why don't we go and see it?'

Twenty minutes later they arrived outside the front gates.

'That's it!' Nick exclaimed. 'That's exactly what I want.'

'But Monsieur Ryman,' Chassagne retorted, a little taken aback. 'It's not on a hill, there are no round towers, no square towers and certainly no turrets. How can you be so sure?'

'I don't know. But it's exactly what I want.'

The recently retired businessman then spoke just three words in English, each one music to the estate agent's ears: 'I'll take it.' And without hesitation he offered the asking price for Château de la Jaubertie: two million francs.

'I think it's fair to say that we both fell in love with Jaubertie together,' Anne explains. 'I loved the château from the first time I saw it. In fact I adored it, especially its shape and neo-Palladian façade, which is quite unusual for the area. We both made up our minds that Jaubertie was *our* house – that it just had to be.'

It is easy to see why. The château, with its escutcheon bearing the Latin motto *'Vide Cui Fides'*, was built from soft golden sandstone towards the end of the sixteenth century by a doctor of the Comte d'Arbois for his mistress, described in the archives simply as a *'danseuse'*. And no less a person than Henri de Navarre, the first Bourbon king of France, was a regular visitor to the château, likewise invariably in the company of his mistress, Gabrielle d'Estrées, the Duchesse de Beaufort, with whom he had become involved during the siege of Chartres and who, of the very many women in his life, exerted the most influence over him. The interior of Jaubertie is all parquet floors, stone staircases and painted ceilings, one of which was completed by a pupil of Nicolas Poussin, a leader of pictorial classicism in the Baroque period.

Above all else, though, the history of the château is inextricably bound up with wine-making in the

Bergerac area. As if to underline this symbiotic relationship between Jaubertie and its vines, a number of scenes depicting life in its vineyards during the different seasons have been permanently carved into the façade of the château itself, and the boundaries of its vineyards are clearly marked on maps dating back to the eighteenth century. The commune of Colombier was once known as Colombier de Monbazillac, highlighting the importance of the magnificently austere and imposing Château de Monbazillac, which dominates the entire Dordogne valley above Bergerac, famed for the 'noble rot' of its liquorous golden wines and situated only three kilometres to the north. And in each and every direction around both Jaubertie and Monbazillac there stretches the unrivalled majesty of 'Purple Périgord', where hundreds of separate vineyards cover over 13,000 hectares of rich and fertile land. Hardly surprising, then, that one local road is known simply as the Route des Vins, for the vines themselves extend as far as the eye can see, in many cases gently merging into the hills and valleys before disappearing into the horizon beyond.

As the Rymans inspected the elegant home and twenty-seven hectares of vineyards they hoped would shortly be theirs, there were more pressing matters to attend to than familiarizing themselves with the château's various personnel. That would all come in good time. But they did catch a glimpse of a small boy playing on his own around the château's rather run-down *chais*. He seemed to be a couple of years younger than their own son, Hugh, and they could not help wondering if the two boys might one day become acquainted. The slim, dark-haired child they had spotted running around close to the wine-making area was François Bacco, the son of Agnès and Joseph Bacco, the poor Italian immigrants who still hoped one day to become naturalized as French citizens. At seven and a half François was already familiar with the skills of driving a tractor, albeit seated on his father's lap.

When the Rymans first set foot on the soil of Jaubertie, the Baccos had been there for the best part of seven years. Joseph cherished his job at the château and he gave the owner, the *pied-noir*, or Algerian-born Frenchman, Robert Sauvat more than a fair day's labour, just as he had done for his previous boss, Philippe Van der Molen, during his years of service at nearby St Germain-et-Mons. Now aged thirty-three, he showed no signs that his appetite for hard work had diminished, and he continued to rush around Jaubertie's rows of vines at a pace which put every other worker to shame. He was happy to have secured for himself everything he held dear: regular employment, a respectable wage and decent living accommodation in the *métairie*, a single-storey outbuilding in the grounds of the château with magnificent views of the Dordogne valley all around. But when Joseph first heard rumours that Jaubertie might be for sale, he immediately felt threatened and insecure. Sauvat might have been strict and even at times entirely unreasonable, but at least his behaviour had the advantage of certainty. Who could tell what changes a new regime might bring? Aware that it would have been inappropriate for him to ask his employer outright, Joseph began to wonder whether or not his days at Jaubertie might be numbered.

And yet Agnès had never been more content. As she basked in the joys of motherhood, her faith in the Almighty was stronger than ever. The reason for this was not at all difficult to detect, for on 5 April 1965, sixteen months after the birth of her son, her prayers had finally been answered, and she had been blessed with a daughter, Claudine. And what a fuss she made of her, spending in Bergerac's market every centime she could spare in kitting out *la petite* in the very best clothes and shoes she could afford.

Eventually Joseph decided that he could hold his tongue no longer. There were too many comings and goings taking place at Jaubertie for his liking, each visit more unsettling than the next. It was imperative, if only for his own peace of mind, that he find out precisely what was going on. He decided to ask Antoine Catalan, the château's resident *régisseur* (manager), if he might approach Monsieur Sauvat on his behalf. Bacco's question was quite straightforward: was it or was it not the case that the château was likely to be sold? The answer, relayed to Bacco via his fellow Italian intermediary, was precisely what he had suspected and served only to exacerbate his worst fears. Yes, Sauvat had replied, should he be offered a sufficiently attractive price, then he was indeed minded to dispose of Jaubertie. And it soon became apparent that in Monsieur Ryman Sauvat was convinced that he had found a prospective purchaser without parallel, a person whose desire to acquire Château de la Jaubertie was surpassed only by his readiness to accept an ever-increasing asking price.

And yet Sauvat had problems of his own with which

A VINEYARD IN THE DORDOGNE

to contend. The most pressing of these undoubtedly
related to his wife, Marie. For Madame Sauvat was
adamant that she would never part with Jaubertie.
During twelve years of residence there, ever since her
hasty exit from Algeria following the insurrection in that
country, she had come to be enchanted with both the
château and its environs. In addition, it had long been
her hope that her teenage son would in due course
follow in her husband's footsteps and take over the
running of the vineyard, then producing white wine
mainly coming from the Sémillon grape and a red
exclusively from Merlot, although neither had proved a
success, with the entire harvest always being sold *en vrac*.
The mere fact that her son showed not the slightest
interest in any aspect of wine-making did not deter
Madame Sauvat from actively pursuing this ambition on
his behalf.

Not surprisingly, such radically differing perspectives
on their future at Jaubertie were hardly conducive to a
harmonious marriage. But rather than choosing to
confront Madame Sauvat directly, Monsieur concluded
that he would be able to operate more effectively if he
acted alone, in the hope that his wife would eventually
come round to his point of view, although the evidence

of her ever having done so in the past was slender indeed. Thus every time the Sauvats travelled south to Aix-en-Provence, to stay at their holiday home in the sunny, tree-lined medieval capital of Provence, Sauvat would quietly give the nod to René Chassagne, the eager estate agent, that the time was now right for prospective purchasers to view. It was into this conjugal confusion that the Rymans had unwittingly stumbled.

On returning from Aix after the Rymans' visit and having acquainted herself with her husband's antics, Madame Sauvat made it quite clear that she was not at all amused. The following day the English couple's offer of two million francs was refused outright. It was left to the unfortunate estate agent, who now saw his commission slipping from his grasp, to be the bearer of the bad news. Under no circumstances would Madame Sauvat sell Jaubertie, he explained reluctantly.

With that unambiguous message ringing in their ears, the Rymans were left with little alternative but to look elsewhere. Redoubling their efforts to find a suitable vineyard, this time they embarked on a search lasting eight months. But every estate they inspected did not compare favourably at all with the one they had already seen. Both of them knew perfectly well what had happened – having worked its magic upon them, Château de la Jaubertie had them hooked.

'Supposing I was to pay a bit more,' Nick ventured to ask Chassagne. 'Do you think that would help matters along at all? What about two and a half million francs?'

'Ah,' Chassagne replied, giving little away. 'I'll put that to my client.'

François Bacco was naturally unaware of the worries weighing heavily on his father's mind. For the young boy Jaubertie was paradise itself, with wonderful woods all around to explore, an old windmill tucked away in the grounds – the perfect place for a game of hide-and-seek – and frequent outings with his father to fish and shoot. It was a healthy, outdoor environment and, in stark contrast to the more cerebral *fils du patron*, François knew from a very early age that he would be only too happy one day to be offered employment as an *ouvrier* at Jaubertie. With his satchel loaded with books, he would walk through the grounds of the château on his way to primary school in the adjoining hamlet of Labadie, tucked away behind the tiny *mairie* (town hall), his parents always confident that he was entirely safe as he strolled through the adjacent woodlands and rows of vines.

The Baccos' son soon learned that Monsieur Sauvat was a man who demanded and received respect. Woe betide the person, little François not excepted, who chose to walk along the edge rather than the middle of a particular pathway, thereby increasing the possibility of spilling pebbles on to the owner's hallowed lawn. With his employees Sauvat could be harsher still: there would only ever be one warning in respect of work deemed to be unsatisfactory – a conversation that would lead to just one thing – the sack. But Madame Sauvat was capable of showing great kindness to the Bacco children, although they did not always perceive it as such, making a point of giving François and Claudine one hour's instruction in the basic tenets of Catholicism every Wednesday, on their day off from school.

The Rymans' son was a much more troubled soul than young François Bacco. Having been sent off to boarding school in England from the age of nine, Hugh was singularly ill at ease in the strange new world in which he suddenly found himself and where, he soon discovered, the law of the jungle prevailed.

'It was from that moment of being sent away that my relationship with the family broke up. And that rift has continued to exist ever since. I am sure that my parents meant well, but it wasn't right for me and I hold both of them to blame in equal measure. I very much resented the fact that my sisters were not sent away, more so Corinne because she was closer to my age. This was made all the worse because our schools were close to one another. I felt it was wrong that my family was so near and yet so far. Eventually I learned how to become independent and survive on my own, but I never really took to the public school world of prefects, punishments, beds being turned upside down, not to mention the bullying. I remember crying when I was split up from my family for the first time. The first and second time that they left I used to kiss them goodbye. But after that you didn't do it any more.'

With other matters on their minds, Nick and Anne Ryman were unaware of the anguish being endured by their son. Eighteen months had passed and they were still no nearer to purchasing Jaubertie. Their offer of two and a half million francs had been turned down. As was a subsequent offer of three million.

'This was during the early seventies,' Nick explains, 'when inflation was galloping away and everyone was buying everything in sight. People didn't know that the oil shock was just around the corner. In 1973, after two years of the Sauvats blowing hot and cold, I was told that if I would like to offer four million francs then it might be considered. I knew that a lot of money still had to be spent on the château – but I thought it was beautiful, quite beautiful. So I said, "All right, offer four million."'

It was double the original asking price, and this time the answer came back that the Sauvats were prepared to sell. With her son's eyes now firmly set on a career in medicine, Madame Sauvat had apparently accepted that the time had come to move on. At least now she would be able to do so in considerable comfort. Nick was informed that he should prepare to attend a meeting towards the end of September at a notary's office in Saussignac, a small village just outside of Bergerac, when the *acte définitif* would be signed.

The Rymans had experienced no such problems in purchasing their new home in England. Quite the contrary. With ample funding to finance their projects, they had invested in The Dye House, a beautiful home in Thursley, near Godalming in Surrey. It might not have been classified as a château, yet it was a most impressive property, with forty-three acres of grounds and a stream. Anne Ryman also had her work cut out, for she purchased and converted some stables at the back of

The Dye House into a going concern, and soon found herself managing both an indoor riding school and a sanctuary for sick ponies. Nick's strategy was simplicity itself: once the sale of the château went through, he would spend one week in England at The Dye House and one week in France at Jaubertie. Like that he would have the best of both worlds. Or so he thought.

The Rymans' move from Hertfordshire to Surrey had signalled the beginning of a weakening of the bonds between the two brothers, who had forged such an effective partnership together over the previous two decades. Suddenly, with the business disposed of and their homes further apart, the intimacy began to fade. The Rymans of Hertfordshire were interested in boats. The Rymans of Surrey were not. The Rymans of Surrey were preoccupied by horses. The Rymans of Hertfordshire were not. And although they had previously been able to discuss anything and everything together, Nick had hardly bothered to relate to Desmond the story of his ongoing battle to acquire Jaubertie. It was the beginning of a distancing process which would only continue to grow.

On the morning of Saturday, 29 September 1973 Nick Ryman arrived at the notary's office with all the relevant paperwork and well aware that he was about to pay over the odds for Château de la Jaubertie. By 10 a.m. the vendors had arrived and the proceedings were set to begin. The Sauvats began by addressing the notary and after a few moments their communication was translated to Nick. Their message was entirely consistent with their past method of doing business: 'Monsieur and Madame Sauvat do not think that you are paying them enough money for the château.'

'Well,' the prospective purchaser replied, 'if they are not satisfied, then I have just enough time to catch the afternoon flight back from Bordeaux. Tell them that they have got fifteen minutes to make up their minds.'

And this time Nick meant it. Their surprise might well have come a little late in the day, but he succeeded in calling the Sauvats' bluff, for after much huffing and puffing and waving of arms they managed to come to a decision within the deadline. The price of four million francs was acceptable after all. The notary then went through the detailed clauses set out in the contract, and at a quarter past one Nick signed. Robert Sauvat did likewise. The notary then looked up towards Marie Sauvat, gesturing with a nod that the final signature required was hers.

'I will never sign to sell Château de la Jaubertie,' she announced, to the consternation of all those present. And with those words she picked up the notary's pen and hurled it across the table.

It pained him to have to humiliate his wife so publicly, but her behaviour now left Sauvat with no alternative. Having anticipated his wife's tantrum, he now moved to resolve the matter once and for all. Under the terms of their marriage contract Jaubertie belonged to him; it was as simple as that. And with a flourish he produced a carefully drafted power of attorney authorizing him to proceed with the sale with or without his wife's consent. As Madame Sauvat sat silently seething with fury while struggling to maintain her composure, the transaction was duly completed according to the letter of the law.

Nick rushed to the nearest phone. Anne had to be the first to hear the good news.

'Darling? Sit down. I've got something important to tell you. We've bought the place. It's finally gone through.'

'I remember thinking,' Nick recalls, 'you made up your mind, Ryman, twenty years ago to do this. Now your moment has come. This doesn't happen to many people in respect of their dreams. It was a most exhilarating feeling too – the excitement of starting off something completely new.'

So exciting, in fact, that by the time he arrived back in Bergerac, he was quite unable to concentrate on anything at all. Returning to his car, he wondered what to do next. And as he did so his foot slipped off the clutch, propelling the vehicle into the town's war memorial and denting its freshly painted black iron railings. It was not the sort of fresh start which he had had in mind.

As the new and previous owners of Jaubertie shook hands outside the notary's offices, Sauvat had played a parting shot.

'I think you ought to know that we also have *un fantôme*.'

'A what?' replied Nick, who had still to master the French language.

'The building has a ghost.'

'That's absolutely marvellous,' said Nick. 'That's all I have ever wanted – a lovely old house with high ceilings, on top of a hill, and with a ghost to boot. Tell me, is it male or female?'

'I don't know,' Sauvat retorted, surprised by such an enthusiastic response on the part of the Englishman. The confused expression on Sauvat's face indicated that he had clearly been expecting the new owner to collapse with fear.

'But you will soon find out,' he continued, 'that it walks about between the first and second floors, often dragging furniture about on its way.'

Nick must have been the only City gent in the whole of France that Saturday, dressed in his stiff white collar, tailor-made double breasted grey flannel suit, bowler hat and rolled umbrella tucked under his left arm. But now, with the object of his visit successfully completed, he was preparing to fly back to London.

'Can I suggest that you come to the château tomorrow?' Sauvat intervened, sensing the imminent departure of the man who had just secured his financial future. 'Come along tomorrow at 3 o'clock, and I will give you a few tips about the running of Jaubertie.'

It was a difficult invitation to refuse. The following day, dressed in newly purchased casual clothes, Nick arrived at the château five minutes early, as is his wont.

Joseph Bacco was also there that Sunday, as was little François. The tough, dependable workhorse appeared to be considerably less strained than during recent weeks. The reason for this was not unrelated to the fact that Monsieur Sauvat had informed him that he was to receive a pay rise as from the following day, 1 October. What he had not bothered to communicate to him, however, was that someone else would be picking up the tab. But Joseph was about to find that out for himself.

'Allow me to introduce you to your new *patron*,' Sauvat told him, pointing to Nick. And as far as Joseph was concerned, that was the beginning and end of their consultation in respect of the change of regime at Jaubertie. He then returned to the vineyards with all of his earlier anxieties rekindled, more uncertain than ever as to what the future might bring. It was as well that there was much work waiting to be done, for work invariably warded off his worries and woes. Sauvat then turned to Nick once more. He had something else to say.

'Oh, and by the way, the harvest begins tomorrow.'

GOD SAVE JAUBERTIE! 5

WHILE THE GRACE of Château de la Jaubertie was
beyond dispute, its *chais* were a far from impressive sight.
Dirty, dilapidated and in a state of some disrepair, the
wine-making area had as its centrepiece a rusty old
continuous press. All the vats were made from cement and
had not been cleaned inside or painted outside since
shortly before the Second World War. The two pumps
had been purchased thirty years before that. There was no
earth or plaque filter and no equipment with which to
bottle the wine. Outside, the vineyard appeared to be
equally chaotic. Of the twenty-seven productive hectares
only twenty-two were mature, and of these seven more in

their first season or two of *appellation contrôlée* (guaranteed vintage) age. The policy appeared to have been to plant pockets of different vine varieties in the same row, with Sémillon, Sauvignon Blanc, Merlot and Grenache often growing alongside one another. It was, in short, a shambles.

Not that Nick Ryman was the world's leading authority on wine. Far from it. Just as well, then, that he had taken the trouble to take with him to France a book which he insisted on referring to as *The Happy Man's Guide to How to Run a Vineyard*, although its correct title was *The Science and Technique of Wine*. The book had been published in 1965, and its author, Lionel Frumkin, complained loudly in the preface of the difficulties he had experienced as a student in his search for suitable books written in English which dealt with the technical study of wine. His grievance seemed to be entirely justified, for there were none. The French had a phrase for such a predicament, he explained, *aller aux vendanges sans panier* (going to the harvest without a basket) – a metaphor for unpreparedness. Reading those words Ryman realized that he was rather basketless himself, for the truth was that despite an active and longstanding interest in the tasting, drinking, collecting and informed discussion of wine, he remained entirely ignorant as to how to produce the alcoholic beverage itself. But he could at least draw some comfort from the fact that Frumkin's words of wisdom were there to guide him on his way, laden with cubic capacities and algebraic formulae though they were.

'We thought that the whole process of wine-making was going to be rather easy,' Anne Ryman admits. 'That the sun shone, the grapes grew and got ripe, you picked and then put them in the vat – and that Nick's little red book then told you all about the fermenting and what to do after that.'

Sensing the *naïveté* of Nick Ryman in almost every aspect of oenology, Sauvat moved quickly in an attempt to dispose of his sizeable stock of unsold wine lying in the cellars of Jaubertie, each bottle bearing the château's distinctive label. For was not the perfect purchaser standing there before him that Sunday, the last day of his fourteen-year stay in the Dordogne?

'I said, "No, thank you, I don't want that. I want to start with a clean sheet,"' Nick recalls. 'I might not have been a connoisseur but you didn't need to be to tell that what he was trying to sell me was awful. The dry white was the colour of old onion skins – and his red undrinkable.'

Undeterred by Nick's unflattering assessment of his

wine, Sauvat chanced his luck again. Then what about buying his Peugeot 404 estate? – a snip, he ventured to suggest, at the knock-down price of 8000 francs. Sauvat's logic was not without foundation, for if the Englishman had been prepared to pay twice the original asking price to acquire Jaubertie, then he could think of no good reason why he should not do likewise for his battered old car; nor did he make any mention of the 250,000 kilometres on the clock. But it was another firm if somewhat heavily accented *'non merci'*.

Having booked himself in for a stay of five weeks at the Cyrano, Bergerac's best hotel, named after the eponymous hero of Edmond Rostand's play and the only establishment in town with a restaurant boasting one gourmet star, Nick set off early the following morning in search of some thirty *vendangeurs*. Before long a group of Vietnamese women, muttering away in their mother tongue and bedecked in pointed wicker coolie hats, together with an assortment of Spanish, Portuguese and Italian workers, were fanning out around the château's extensive vineyards, sharpened secateurs in hand, ready to remove the ripe bunches of grapes which had grown during the spring and summer months.

While finding these casual labourers was not a

particularly difficult task – most lived in a poor and predominantly immigrant part of Bergerac called Bikini – feeding them called for detailed planning and preparation. For a number of years this task had fallen to Madame Yvonne Ayral, a plump, elderly woman whose popularity was always impressively high among the *vendangeurs* themselves, owing to her unique style of tasty French country cuisine. Having introduced herself to the proud new owner of Jaubertie, she promptly handed him a piece of paper setting out her culinary requirements, requesting that the items be available an hour or so later that morning. After scanning his dictionary to translate the greater part of the list, Nick headed off towards Bouniagues, situated on the *Route nationale* 21, where the nearest local shops were to be found.

It was immediately upon his return that Antoine Catalan, the resident *régisseur*, approached. The little Italian required a word with the new *patron*. Like his compatriot Joseph Bacco, he had been pondering the consequences of a change of ownership.

'What sort of wine do you want us to make?' he enquired.

'I don't quite understand why you are asking that,' Nick replied, a little bemused. 'There are the vines – aren't we going to make wine out of those vines?'

The *régisseur* paused for a moment before answering. He was not at all sure what to make of this lanky, blue-eyed, fair-haired Englishman, who seemed to be so eager and yet so naïve at the same time. 'Yes, we are,' he replied, doing his utmost to conceal the superior tone of an expert talking down to the most junior of trainees. His eyes, deeply set into an angular, almost foxy face, occasionally gave the impression of moving independently of one another. 'But it's a question of what type you want. Do you want dry white, or sweet white? Or do you want *rosé* or red?'

'Ah. That's a very good question,' said Nick defensively, realizing that he had been caught unawares. From the very first moment of their meeting, he had taken an instant dislike both to the appearance and attitude of the *régisseur*. 'I'll come back to you on that in a short while,' he said, stalling for time.

Retreating to a quiet spot in the grounds of Jaubertie, Nick sat down on a stone and wondered what sort of wine would be likely to fare best on the English market. With not a single statistic to back him up, and nothing more elaborate to rely upon than his hunch, he came to the conclusion that he would be able to sell more dry white than sweet, and more red than *rosé*. He was soon back before the *régisseur*, rattling out the orders which he had hastily conceived.

'I want you to make 150 hectolitres of sweet white wine – all the rest dry. And 150 hectolitres of rosé – all the rest red.'

'In that case we have a problem,' said Catalan. 'There's no difficulty at all concerning the red or *rosé*. But if you want us to make 150 hectolitres of Monbazillac, our sweet white, then you have first got to go and buy a lot of sugar.'

'Why? Is there a shortage of sugar? Is it desperately expensive?'

'No, it's not that. It's just that we need to add sugar and to do that you have to get a piece of paper first.'

'Well, then let's get off and get the piece of paper,' the Englishman snapped, not relishing the prospect of another brush with French bureaucracy.

The *régisseur* then set out his case more clearly, explaining that the grapes were showing only between seven and eight degrees of natural sugar, whereas a minimum of thirteen was required before they could be authorized to make Monbazillac. Unless, that was, the *vigneron* (wine-grower) had previously obtained permission to supplement the wine's level of sweetness and alcohol. That was where the official slip of paper came in. But Nick had heard enough, and he intervened to cut Catalan short.

'Well, that's quite simple then. In that case we don't start at all.'

'There is a way, though,' the *régisseur* ventured to suggest, in the tones of one familiar with every trick of the trade. 'We go to the black market.' And as he whispered those words Catalan lowered both his eyelids and his voice, as if to impress upon the new owner the clandestine nature of the operation he had in mind.

The *régisseur* then sought to further outline the intricacies of the system. If the person concerned had already been authorized to add sugar, then he simply walked into the shop clutching the requisite piece of paper and paid for the merchandise by cheque. But if, like Monsieur Ryman, he had not, then the sugar could be acquired *sans papiers* and paid for in cash. And just to confuse matters still further it soon became apparent that it was the same person in the same shop responsible for the handling of all transactions, both official and unofficial. Returning to his room at the Cyrano Hotel, the rather baffled new proprietor of Château de la Jaubertie began to wonder for the first time precisely what he had let himself in for. Peeling off a number of hundred-franc notes and folding them neatly into an unmarked brown envelope, Nick could not help thinking what old Frumkin would have had to say about it all.

Throughout the month of that harvest Madame Ayral was adamant that Monsieur Ryman should not eat lunch with the *vendangeurs*, insisting instead that he should do so with her once the workers had completed their meal. It was simply not the done thing, she explained, for the château owner to be seen to be rubbing shoulders with those in his employ, although there was clearly room for the odd exception such as herself.

From the outset she assumed responsibility for ensuring that Nick's gastronomic requirements were catered for, and towards the end of the first week she enquired as to his plans for the coming weekend. With his wife still in England running The Dye House and looking after both Camilla and Corinne, he had nothing particular in mind other than to catch up on some sleep.

'No,' Madame Ayral said, 'you'll come to lunch with me, in my house. My husband and I would be delighted to entertain you.'

'We started with oysters,' Nick remembers. 'And then

we had *pâté de foie gras*, followed by *omelette aux cèpes*, and then we had *confit de canard rôti*. That was followed by Roquefort, and then salad, rounding off with her *tarte aux pommes* – and all the accompanying wines with each dish. It was an absolute feast. Delicious, the whole thing.'

That was considerably more than could be said for the wines of Jaubertie, though this unhappy state of affairs was not unrelated to the fact that Catalan had still to declare his hand. For throughout the period of his employment by Monsieur and Madame Sauvat he had been the beneficiary of a two-franc incentive for every hectolitre of wine produced, in accordance with a policy of quantity at the expense of quality. And since nothing had been said to the contrary, he had taken the liberty of assuming that the terms of his contract of employment, although undiscussed, remained unchanged. Hardly surprising then that that year's Monbazillac was not quite the sensation for which Nick had been hoping.

'It ended up as the most ghastly lemonade I have ever tasted in my entire life. So I sold the whole lot to a *négociant*, which barely covered the cost of the sugar.'

The harvest ended with another of Madame Ayral's magnificent meals. This time Nick was allowed to join in the fun, on the grounds that it was *la fête* all round. The *vendangeurs* were eating, drinking and singing, satisfied that they had worked well and been remunerated reasonably enough. And then all of a sudden the room fell silent, with every eye apparently focusing on Monsieur Ryman himself. Nor did he have to be familiar with any of his workers' numerous languages to understand precisely what was expected of him: it was the turn of *le patron* to come up with a song. Shy and self-effacing by nature, despite the aggressive commercial role he had occasionally assumed during his years at the helm in the stationery business, Nick was not at all sure what to do. But mindful that it would be better to get the deed over, slowly he began. With the large Vietnamese contingent gazing up at him uncomprehendingly, he could think of nothing more appropriate than to deliver a rendition of 'God Save the Queen' – and everybody immediately appeared to be satisfied with that. He might well have added 'God Save Château de la Jaubertie', for the fact of the matter was that the only thing which that year's harvest had so far produced was sustained financial loss.

For a man whose ambition was to make the best wine in Bergerac it was not an impressive start. And yet the *terroir*, the soil of Jaubertie, the most important factor determining the character of each wine, had much to commend it. A limestone plateau rising up to an altitude of 170 metres above the valley of the Dordogne, its profile is rendzina with a soft clay topsoil, ideal for retaining moisture during the long and hot dry summers. Protected from the prevailing south-west winds by long lines of fir, lime and acacia trees, the vineyard also benefited from a microclimate which conferred a number of further advantages, including excellent exposure to sunlight. Given his readiness to invest in the infrastructure of his asset, all that Nick Ryman required was the presence of trained personnel to properly exploit his domain. But the fact was, he was being exploited himself. For the contents of an entire *cuve* (vat), the equivalent of some 7,000 bottles of wine, had somehow managed to vanish into thin air. Even Madame Ayral's husband, a conjuror by profession, was incapable of performing such a feat. There was only one man who could possibly have been responsible, Ryman reasoned, and the finger of suspicion immediately fell upon Antoine Catalan, who soon found himself earmarked for early retirement, and thus ceasing to be the château's resident *régisseur*. Catalan did not seek to create too much of a stir about such an ignominious end to his career, however, for not only did he receive a generous financial settlement, but he also happened to have two freehold properties of his own to choose between when deciding on his future accommodation – most unusual for a worker on an agricultural wage.

Not long after Catalan's departure René Chassagne appeared unexpectedly at Jaubertie. The estate agent was more than a little curious to find out how his former client was getting on. As they exchanged the preliminary courtesies he sensed that the Englishman was feeling a little downcast.

'I want to ask you one question,' he said. 'Do you know how to make wine?'

'Quite honestly, I do not know the first thing,' Nick replied, clearly ready to unburden himself, and paying scant regard to the very many lessons he had learned since his arrival at Jaubertie.

'That's what I thought,' Chassagne commented. 'What I would like to do, if you will permit me, is to introduce you to a dear old man I know. His name is Jean Rigal and he is seventy-five years old. He's a very competent wine-maker who once had his own vineyard and I am sure that if I had a word with him he would be prepared to help out.'

It was a difficult offer to refuse. Within a few days Jean Rigal, whose own vineyard had been almost entirely wiped out during the 1956 frost, was conducting a tour of inspection of the *chais* of Jaubertie. Ten minutes later he emerged with two handfuls of crushed grapes.

'That's what they've been doing,' he said triumphantly, and with the authority of one who had spent a lifetime among *les vignes*. 'Screwing up that press so tightly that you haven't been making wine at all.'

Releasing the pressure of the press also revealed that it had only ever been cleaned by putting grapes through it. Everything Rigal had to say seemed to be consistent with the *régisseur's* policy, apparently sanctioned by the Sauvats, of orienting the vineyard towards the bulk production of grapes, with scant regard to quality and still less to the most elementary notions of hygiene.

'I'll help you with the vinification this year,' said the old man. 'But what you must do is find yourself a qualified oenologist. And preferably one from the ENSA, the École Nationale Supérieure d'Agronomie in Montpellier. You must then ensure that that person comes to be based permanently at Jaubertie. That is if you really are serious about making good wine.'

Henry Mondié, working on his uncle's farm in Mexico, was in a quandary. For it was while in that country that he had first heard about the possibility of a position at Jaubertie, via the good offices of his friend Jean Abeille, chairman of the association of former ENSA students. Yet he was hardly going to rush back to France while matters remained so vague; nor was the prospect of bringing a premature end to his prolonged honeymoon particularly appealing. Nick Ryman had replied to Henry's initial enquiry by asking him to come along for an interview, true enough, but the young ENSA graduate took the not unreasonable view that he might also have asked a couple of dozen other candidates to do likewise. He decided that before taking the issue any further the best thing to do would be to embark upon an intelligence-gathering exercise. And with that in mind he asked his sister-in-law, Lydie Cazaubiel, the most unlikely of spies but somebody who happened to live only thirty kilometres away in the neighbouring *département* of Lot et Garonne, to find out about Jaubertie for him. When she reported how very attractive were both the château and its grounds, Henry decided that it was no longer sensible to hedge his bets and duly presented himself for an interview in October 1973. A few days later he received written confirmation that he had succeeded in securing the post. He was delighted, and so was his wife.

'For my first year or so at Jaubertie I was more or less alone,' Henry recalls. 'Monsieur Ryman would come every month or so just to oversee. He told me that he wanted to make fine wine – but he didn't have the equipment with which to make it. Whenever I would put projects to him, though, he would always reply with the same phrase: "I want the best."'

This was no idle big talk on the part of the former Ryman boss. For before long plans were being drawn up to redesign the *chais*, to replace the old cement *cuves* with the latest stainless-steel variety, and to buy an earth filter and a simple bottling machine. Money, it seemed, was no object. Nor did Nick's plans stop at the purchase of materials. Insisting that he wanted to concentrate on making very good quality dry white wine, he gave the go-ahead for a major programme of replanting of some of the older vines with Sauvignon Blanc, a grape which makes a distinctive aromatic and occasionally smoky-scented wine. No more favouring of quantity over quality now. Quite the reverse.

'Apart from my trip to Mexico,' Henry remembers,

'moving to the Bergerac area was really my first time out
of the Midi. Monsieur Ryman gave me *carte blanche* and in
terms of materials I got whatever I wanted. I had a lot of
responsibility and I was proud of what we were setting
out to achieve. I became completely involved in my work
to the point sometimes of showing somebody around
and referring to Jaubertie as 'ours'. Since there were no
secretaries or accountants to handle the paperwork, I
would often take documents home with me and work late
into the night, which I didn't mind in the slightest. It was
my first proper job and I was determined to make it a
great success.'

In fact Henry was more than happy to have something
to do with himself in the evenings after dark. Separated
from his young bride, who continued to teach student
nurses in Narbonne, he had agreed with Gabrielle that
the most sensible thing to do was to bide their time for a
while before committing themselves to the purchase of a
house in the area. The eager oenologist therefore rented
a modest single room in Bouniagues, at the tiny Hôtel
des Voyageurs, just a five-minute drive from Jaubertie.
More often than not he was the only guest staying there,
and he soon found himself spending more than the
occasional evening chatting with Monsieur and Madame

Feytou, the hospitable *propriétaires*. Speaking one evening about her student days, only recently completed, Madame told Henry that she had herself once been in lodgings in Narbonne. When she mentioned a student nurse with whom she would often travel to and from Narbonne, his ears at once pricked up.

'And what was the name of that person?' he asked.

'Gabrielle Montez.'

'Well, that young lady,' Henry replied, 'is now my wife.'

Within six months of acquiring Jaubertie Nick had come to the conclusion that his original idea of running the vineyard on a part-time basis was no longer viable. It probably never was. His experience with the *régisseur* had taught him that. It was clear that the Rymans were going to have to make up their minds between The Dye House and Jaubertie. With Hugh back from boarding school for the whole of the Easter holidays, a family conference was called. It did not last very long. For everybody's hands immediately shot up in favour of France.

'You do realize what that means,' Nick said, addressing the three children. 'That you'll have to go through the French educational system and adapt to a different way of life.'

If that comment was designed to set alarm bells ringing in the minds of Hugh, Corinne or Camilla, it evidently failed to do the trick, for there was not a murmur of dissent. The following day The Dye House was in the hands of estate agents, and the lure of Jaubertie stronger than ever.

In the middle of August 1974 five full-sized removal lorries belonging to a firm in Camberley were rumbling through the Pas de Calais, heading south towards the valley of the Dordogne. Anne Ryman, enthused by the adventure before her, drove down in a horse transporter containing Tiger, Knocky and Perry, likewise destined for pastures new. Together with twelve-year-old Hugh, she stopped overnight in Le Havre, intending to arrive in Colombier later the next day. When they did so, Nick was already there, having managed to cram his two daughters, two cats and two dogs into the same car, and all were apparently none the worse for the ordeal.

The following day Camilla, just turned seven, was standing in the elegant *grand salon* on the first floor of Jaubertie when she suddenly spotted the fleet of bright-red removal lorries wending their way towards the château. Sixteen men emerged from the vehicles and in the heat of the summer sun they set about unloading the

Rymans' furniture, clothes and dozens of tea chests containing their lifetime's possessions. A few hours later those same men were cooling off in the swimming pool in the grounds of Jaubertie, having also been invited to stay for lunch.

Anne's parents, Isobel and Bennie Butters, had also travelled to France to help with the move and soon found themselves caught up in the atmosphere of excitement, running round desperately trying to arrange the impromptu lunch. The figures, if not the catering, were easy enough to work out. Five Rymans plus two in-laws plus sixteen ravenous removal men made twenty-three at table.

'By the time we sat down for dinner later that evening something quite extraordinary happened,' Anne reflects. 'In a way it was almost as if we had never moved. Because everything was there at Jaubertie. Everyone was there too. Plus all of the animals. And we all continued to speak English, of course. It felt like we had merely upped and moved the house from England – home from home really.'

The only one having any difficulty integrating, it seemed, was Henry. For the family's English setter wasted little time in registering his disapproval, disappearing into the thick of the night. The gendarmerie was informed without delay, as was the local Société Protectrice des Animaux. Then, three weeks later, when the Ryman children had come to fear the worst, the telephone rang. It was the police.

'We think that we have found your dog, Monsieur Ryman,' a helpful gendarme revealed. He went on to explain that Henry had managed to make his way to Castillonnès, eleven kilometres to the south of Bouniagues on the *nationale* 21. 'It's all right, though,' he insisted. 'You don't need to worry. We have found a retired colonel who is speaking to him in English.'

Even though the Ryman family had little difficulty in settling into their new home, the truth was that Château de la Jaubertie had been much neglected over the years. The basic structure of the building was sound enough, but its roof certainly was not, which explained the presence of some thirty dustbins strategically positioned immediately underneath it, each container requiring a little realignment every time it rained.

One hundred and eighty years earlier it had been a very different story at Jaubertie. Then, during the period of the Revolutionary government, two officials had been dispatched from the district of Bergerac to compile an inventory of the furniture at the château. The noble owner, Albert de la Jaubertie, was not there to greet them, however, having already fled from France in an understandable attempt to avoid the oblique-edged blade of the guillotine, evidently drawing little comfort from the knowledge that the instrument had been introduced with the express purpose of making the process of decapitation as swift and painless as possible. The official inventory ran to many pages, detailing the fine golden-oak furniture and splendid *objets d'art* displayed in the château's fifteen rooms, including 170 paintings set in golden frames, fifteen mirrors, several small pieces sculpted from white marble, three bronzes and an abundance of smaller but equally valuable items. All of which subsequently disappeared in the aftermath of that revolutionary fervour.

Nick did not require anyone to tell him that there was much work to be done at Jaubertie, quite apart from attempting to recapture some of its former splendour. But from the outset his priority was to concentrate on improving the vineyards rather than the château, and the greater part of his energy and expenditure was allocated to that. Not that concentrating on outside improvements could in any way be considered as pursuing the cheap option, for his policy of replanting various vines was an extremely costly business, requiring the passage of at least four or five years before he would see the arrival of any new crop. Still, as long as everything was budgeted for. And who better to tackle such a task than the former financial director of the Ryman empire?

'Actually I did the whole thing flying by the seat of my pants. I didn't bother about costing it out at all. Quite foolishly, I know. But I had had enough of accountants and projections from my Rymans days. So I began to splash out on this and that.'

No wonder Joseph Bacco soon came to give his wholehearted approval to the new regime. With the Rymans installed at Jaubertie, not only had new equipment begun to flow thick and fast, but an altogether friendlier, family atmosphere had come to prevail, in marked contrast to the iron fist of Monsieur Sauvat. Here was a *patron* who not only appeared to accord his employees both dignity and respect, he would also occasionally ask them in to *boire un coup*, whereas taking a drink with the boss was hitherto unknown at Jaubertie. In fact Joseph Bacco shared with Nick Ryman a common interest not just in the production of wine but also in its consumption, and this was perhaps one of the reasons why it did not take too long before the two men, both immigrants to France, were soon singing each other's praises.

Bacco's eleven-year-old son François had reason to be equally content. For in Corinne and Hugh he had found two new children of more or less the same age to play with. The fact that they happened not to share the same language hardly proved a stumbling block, and before that first summer was through they had spent many a day together around the swimming pool at Jaubertie. There was not the remotest hint of any system of apartheid between them; and it never once crossed Hugh's mind to draw a distinction between the *fils de l'ouvrier* and himself, the more privileged *fils du patron*. Nor was Camilla excluded from the friendships being forged during the course of the summer of 1974, for in Claudine Bacco she too had found a willing playmate, just two years her junior. For the Ryman children the Bacco family provided their first real contact with France. It could hardly have gone more smoothly had it been prepared in advance by a learned committee of experts in cultural integration.

Throughout those first few weeks in France Nick was determined that there should never be any mention of the ghost supposed to stalk the upper floors of Jaubertie, hauling around the odd item of furniture *en route*. With the challenges of a new school and a new language before them, the last thing he wanted was for the children to be scared out of their wits, with all of the consequences that could flow from that. He therefore treated the matter like a state secret. But such silence and sensitivity on his part did nothing to prevent it from coming to the attention of the children from their very first days at Jaubertie. For everybody, it seemed, had something to say about *le fantôme*. The Sauvats themselves had spoken darkly about two bodies buried below an office situated in a wing of the château, while others in the area who had lived through the German occupation talked convincingly of a long tunnel running underneath the château where people, objects and food had been hidden throughout the turbulent years of the Second World War.

It was not long before such spooky talk began to linger in the fertile imagination of Camilla, the youngest and most inquisitive of the Rymans' three children. To make matters worse, she was distinctly ill at ease in her new bedroom, which she considered to be oversized, dark and depressing. Was the large crack in its ceiling, she wondered, not a sure sign that it was on the brink of collapsing on her? And were there not likely to be a series of carefully concealed skeletons waiting to emerge from behind closed doors? And yet, despite her manifest fear of an unexpected encounter with the as yet nameless ghost of Jaubertie, Camilla nevertheless secretly hoped to meet him. After much thought she had come to the conclusion that he was likely to be friendly and that she had nothing to fear. Unable to get to sleep at night, she would lie awake wondering what she might say to him should he suddenly decide to appear before her. After all, she reasoned, she would not want to find herself stuck for conversation, although this was a fate which rarely befell her since she had been a most effective communicator from a very early age. With that possibility in mind she would run through a series of imaginary dialogues, each one terribly chatty and polite, so that she would be able to engage her ghostly visitor in conversation.

'Hello,' she would begin. 'My name is Camilla. How are you? I'm very well.'

And so she would continue, talking about herself and making intelligent enquiries of the spirit she had deemed to be her friend, often for some time, until finally she fell asleep.

Yet strange, if not supernatural, events undoubtedly

Top: Nick Ryman at Silverstone in May 1956, driving the Mk 6 Lotus that he bought 'fourteenth hand' and which was subsequently smashed up at the Kent race track by his racing partner. *(Nick Ryman)*

Below left: Nick Ryman and his older brother Desmond in the garden of Sunshine House, Chorleywood, Hertfordshire. *(Nick Ryman)*

Below right: National Service took Nick Ryman, seen here in 1951, to El Kirsh in Egypt, where he became a second lieutenant in the army. *(Nick Ryman)*

Top left: Château de la Jaubertie, built towards the end of the sixteenth century and situated in Colombier, five miles south of Bergerac, depicted in a postcard, date stamped in 1902. *(Nick Ryman)*

Top right: A postcard from the 1930s shows the neo-palladian pediment that replaced the stepped roofline of Château de la Jaubertie sometime during the early part of the century. *(Nick Ryman)*

Below: A triumphant Anne Ryman emerges from Ryman Conran's company helicopter after landing it on HMS *Eagle* in October 1970.

(Nick Ryman)

Nick Ryman would inspect his domain, with its superb views of the
Dordogne valley, by driving around the vineyards in his 1923 Citröen
Kegresse halftrack. *(Nick Ryman)*

The Ryman family and their staff, as pictured by Nick Ryman, during the *vendanges* of 1976, the penultimate wine harvest to use hand pickers. Anne Ryman is in the front row, wearing a dark blouse. On her left is Madame Ayral, the fine cook who, with Anne as her number two, satisfied the appetites of family and *vendangeurs* alike during the wine harvest at Jaubertie. Both women are looking at Henry, the family's much loved

English setter. Sitting at the right-hand end of the stone ledge on the right is Joseph Bacco, who gave the Rymans many years of tireless service. Standing behind Bacco are, from right to left, Hugh, the Rymans' eldest child; Mandy, an English girl who helped for one harvest; Henry Mondié who was the manager of the vineyards; and the Rymans' daughters, Camilla and Corinne.

(Nick Ryman)

Above: Françoise Bacco, son of Joseph and Agnès, was nine months old when the family arrived at Château de la Jaubertie, where he was later to become maître de chais, or cellar master.

(François Bacco)

Right: Jean Rigal enjoys a simple country meal of wine, ham and bread. The retired local wine-maker gave Nick Ryman invaluable help and advice during his first vintage in 1973.

(Nick Ryman)

Italian-born Joseph Bacco stayed on to work in the vineyards, when
Nick Ryman bought Jaubertie from Robert Sauvat, and was later to
become the estate's chef de culture, in charge of the day-to-day
management of the vines. He is seen here in front of an out-building,
in which the Bacco family at one time lived.   *(Nick Ryman)*

Above: Henry Mondié, centre, was instrumental in ensuring the success of Jaubertie's wines under Nick Ryman (standing, left) with his wife, Anne (at the table). The oenologist worked at Jaubertie for nearly eleven years and became the mayor of Colombier. Hugh Ryman stands, with a glass to his lips, behind his wife, Anne. *(Henry Mondié)*

Right: Nick Ryman converted the ground-floor of a small wing of Jaubertie into an attractive breakfast-room overlooking the gardens at the front of the château.

did take place at Jaubertie. For one bright August afternoon, just a few weeks after the arrival of the Rymans, the skies suddenly began to darken. Five minutes later there was little sign of any daylight at all. Then, as if from nowhere, a most almighty storm erupted, with hailstones the size of tomatoes immediately crashing down on the château and its grounds. As Anne busied herself shovelling the hailstones out of her kitchen, Nick set off with Hugh and Corinne to try to find out where the three horses were in case they bolted, fearful of the storm.

The storm took barely twenty minutes to pass, ending as dramatically as it had begun. As they set off to inspect any damage, the first thing which caught the Rymans' attention was the condition of Anne's parents' cream Mercedes coupé, which was parked outside. No expert assessor was required to see that it had sustained damage running into hundreds of pounds, for it was peppered with dents from the impact of the huge hailstones. The storm had brewed up so quickly and the accompanying rain fallen so fast and furiously that Nick had not had time to adjust the dustbins underneath the roof. But that, he soon came to realize, was the last of his worries. Twenty-seven panes of glass had been broken in virtually every part of the château, as if the Rymans' residence had come under sustained enemy fire.

Joseph Bacco then appeared on the scene. So too did Henry Mondié. Both men shrugged their shoulders and shook their heads in disbelief, as if to indicate that they too had difficulty in recalling such a storm. Together with their new *patron* they went straight to the vineyards to see precisely what damage had been done. They soon realized that there was precious little to inspect. Over eighty per cent of the crop had been destroyed, leaves and grapes alike ripped to pieces by the savagery of the storm.

Surveying the sorry sight before him, Nick recalled how, a year earlier, his first wines had been undrinkable. He had vowed never to let that happen again. He had moved the whole family to France so that he could become more closely involved in every aspect of his wine's production. And here was his second year's crop – gone.

MADAME BROUETTE

SHE HAD COME to France thinking that she knew how to cook. As a graduate of the Cordon Bleu Cookery School in London she had good reason to. But Anne Ryman was about to become a born-again cordon bleu. The reason for such a radical reappraisal of her culinary capabilities was Madame Yvonne Ayral, the elderly and rather large French lady retained for the duration of the *vendanges*, who did not have a single diploma in catering to her name.

'I did cook well by English standards. But cooking for the French is something quite different,' says Anne. 'I could see that any one of Madame Ayral's meals was far tastier than anything I could offer. I soon ended up in the kitchen as her number two, helping to serve a four-course lunch for between thirty and forty people every day during the vintage. That was when I realized that I really didn't know anything about cooking at all – it was like starting from scratch. And I began to learn how to prepare classical French country dishes like *lapin aux petits oignons, tripes, lentilles, blanquette de veau*, in addition to all of the soups. I adored this food, because it was much more natural, more wholesome and more home-grown.'

Sensing her readiness to absorb every aspect of French rural life, a neighbouring farmer enquired if Madame Ryman had ever killed a pig. No, she had not. And whether or not she might be interested to find out how to make the various pâtés and sausages once slaughtering had been carried out. 'So off I went and I soon found myself standing in water with pig intestines, washing them out in a stream which ran beside the farm. They had a big black cauldron on the farm in which they cooked *boudin*, blood sausage, and there I was with blood up to my arms making the mixture. I found it all quite fascinating, seeing how the intestines didn't break once you put the meat in because the stream ran so gently. They also taught me how to make the pâtés, the ham and everything else from the pig.'

From that moment on Anne was a convert to the cause and every year the family bought and butchered their own pig at Jaubertie. Percy was the first to go. And he was soon followed by Percy Two, then Percy Three, and so on. Not that Anne enjoyed the brutal and noisy ritual of slaughter. Though hardly squeamish, even she could not bring herself to witness these primitive proceedings. Instead she would discreetly absent herself for a while until she heard that familiar reassuring knock on the door, her cue to emerge from hiding.

'Madame,' a voice would announce, 'il est mort.' Then, in a process which must have remained unchanged throughout the centuries, poor Percy, whatever his number, would be laid out on a racking device next to a huge cauldron of water, before being strung up in the yard, shaved with a large, wooden-handled razor in readiness for the sharp edge of the butcher's knife, with which the deceased swine would then be methodically cut up and in due course transformed into smoked hams, salamis, bacon and an assortment of other joints and chops. Whatever would Anne's refined young contemporaries from the Cordon Bleu Cookery School have made of that?

She might only have been seven, but Camilla Ryman

was astute enough to anticipate that she would be likely to fare better at her new school in France as Camille. And she duly introduced herself as such. If only the rest of the language could have been handled with equivalent ease. But Camilla, although considered by her parents as their child with the greatest facility with words, immediately found that she was barely able to express herself in French. Excluded by her classmates, she was relieved that an extremely sympathetic teacher was on hand to assist. Seeing how the most recent member of her class was being simultaneously shunned and ignored, the *maîtresse* would rebuke her pupils for failing to make any effort to befriend the new girl. *'Vous pouvez parler à Camille'* ('You can speak to Camilla'), she would exhort. It was undoubtedly well-intentioned, though from Camilla's point of view the notion that children might suddenly be speaking to her because they had been told to do so, or threatened with dire consequences if they did not, only made matters worse.

The most common consequence of Camilla's feelings of isolation and exclusion was an urgent telephone call from the school's headmistress to her mother at Jaubertie. 'Could somebody please come and collect Camille right away because she is complaining of a headache?' The following day it was as likely to be a tummy upset, for Camilla had the wit to deploy a repertoire of imaginary maladies. And so it went on throughout the first month at school. *'Vous êtes tous très méchants, excepté Camille'* ('You're all very naughty except for Camilla'), the teacher would occasionally call out, exasperated – another of her phrases which served only to heighten the separateness of *la petite anglaise*. Six months later, however, it was a very different story. Fluent in French, top in grammar, Camilla had worked her way up to third position overall, and proudly claimed her place in the front row among the brightest and best of the class. The great communicator had lived up to her reputation after all.

Corinne had not been on hand to help Camilla, having been sent to a private school run by a holy order of nuns in Bergerac. This was not as a consequence of any desire of the Rymans to suddenly instil religious values in their elder daughter, but merely because the local state-run *collège* (secondary school) had declared that it had neither the time nor the resources to begin teaching English children the intricacies of French. The result of this linguistic exclusion order was that Corinne found herself attending La Miséricorde, a school whose name matched her melancholy feelings towards this rather austere seat of learning. Like Camilla she suffered a great deal during the first few months, and she would spend part of each day attempting to fend off the tears constantly welling up inside her. Desperately wanting to be one of the crowd but unable as yet to belong, she soon changed from an effusive and outgoing young girl into a shy and introverted personality, embarrassed by her own ineptitude in French and given to blushing repeatedly throughout the day. Away from the classroom, she longed for the more horse-oriented culture of middle-class England, missing the shows and gymkhanas in which previously she had participated almost every weekend. Thank goodness for the one constant companion in her life, Champagne Perry, half-horse, half-pony, and an excellent jumper too: at least he was always there to offer love, comfort and reassurance.

'The fact that I would no longer be a boarder was definitely my first reason for wanting to go to France,' Hugh Ryman admits. 'And secondly to follow the family. I felt that I would be more free. I was on the point of being sent off to my new school – Milton Abbey –

where a place was being kept open for me. So it was either France or public school. Once at Jaubertie I still didn't completely reintegrate into the family, though. That had been broken up by my having been sent away to boarding school at the age of nine.'

Hugh also found himself stationed in Bergerac, at St Front, another *école religieuse*. He had had the good fortune to have already made contact with another boy in his class, Bertrand Duc, who kindly took him under his wing. But even that protective gesture could not assist Hugh in understanding what was being said in class, despite French having been his strongest subject while at school in England. Yet he still managed to scrape through his BEPC examinations, roughly equivalent to GCSE, after just two terms, and that despite a mark of nought out of twenty for French dictation. Just as well, then, that his eighteen in English had been able to redress the balance.

'It was all very different from my English public school,' Hugh remembers. 'My world had changed, but for the better. My shyness still prevailed, but most of the boys were quite nice with me. You were no longer shut up in your little kingdom of prep school; to me it felt as if I was discovering the real world – freedom – watching

TV at home, going out walking. I was just discovering ordinary everyday things of life – living. And I was much happier because of that.'

Hugh's father seemed to be a much happier man too. In fact Nick had much in common with his children in that he was also receiving daily instruction, albeit outside a formally structured academic environment. Under the guidance of his energetic young oenologist Henry Mondié, he was pressing full steam ahead with a programme of modernization and replanting, despite the series of disasters which had befallen him, and all the time being more convinced of the importance of temperature control in wine-making. With that in mind he proceeded with the purchase of a cooling machine in order to follow a process of cold fermentation. By keeping the temperature to 18°C, he noticed an immediate improvement in his dry white wines, particularly in their fruitiness and bouquet. Stainless-steel fermenting vats were also soon standing proudly at Jaubertie. Nick's philosophy might have been anathema to the die-hards of the old school, but his view was that it was better to produce a clean, fresh wine which has been kept under inert gas in stainless steel than a dirty wine tasting of old wood and other more unpleasant things.

In addition he planted high vines in order to allow the maximum use of machinery for cultivation and picking, thereby paving the way for the introduction of automatic picking machines at Jaubertie. To Nick the greatest advantage of these, that of timing, seemed all too apparent. For whereas previously *vignerons* were often obliged to start picking before the grapes were at their best and likewise to finish a week or so later than they might otherwise have wished, it suddenly became possible to pick a particular type of grape on the ideal day and at ideal temperatures too. And he marvelled at the larger and more sophisticated machines which he had watched in operation in the Médoc, racing up and down the rows of vines and cropping at a speed which would have called for the manual skills of at least 150 *vendangeurs*.

But by no means did every aspect of wine-making at Jaubertie suddenly become computer-controlled or high-tech. In a process which invariably involved every member of the family, Nick would periodically produce an old car windscreen, over which a generous layer of glue had been spread. Labels would then be laid out on the sticky glass, before being applied to each bottle by hand. The efforts of children and adults alike were frequently rejected by a straightforward system of quality control which demanded simply that a label should be the right way up and aligned properly with the sides of the bottle.

What did the locals make of this Englishman in their midst; a man, moreover, who never went out of his way to disguise his determination to produce the best wines both in the Bergerac region and beyond?

'French reaction was probably akin to that of a native of Perth towards a Frenchman making whisky at Blair Atholl,' is Nick's guess. 'In other words that I was a bloody fool. I would put the hostility at about fifty-fifty, although nothing was ever stated, of course. But the undercurrent was that they knew much more about wine-making than I did, and that I ought to have been thrown out from the word go.'

This attitude was exemplified by some local people who asked Monsieur Ryman, not long after his arrival at Château de la Jaubertie, whether or not it was his intention to make the sweet dessert wine of Monbazillac. Of course it was. The locals were not shy to give their opinion as to the wisdom of such a venture.

In short it was a waste of time. They then proceeded to set out what appeared to be a rather convincing case, reminding the new *propriétaire* that his estate was situated on top of the valley, with wide spaces between its vines. These were far from ideal conditions in which to attempt to make a good Monbazillac, they pointed out, for this wine traditionally calls for north-facing slopes lower down a valley, with lower vines planted closer together, so as to get the celebrated noble rot. But since Colombier was one of only five communes entitled to use the Monbazillac *appellation*, a restriction dating back to before the Second World War, Nick was determined not to be discouraged by the doom and gloom merchants. And that in spite of his earlier unsuccessful attempt during the days of his *régisseur* Antoine Catalan. Therefore it was with considerable pride that Henry Mondié and Nick Ryman received the Millésime 1976 Gold Medal for their Monbazillac, just three years after Nick's acquisition of Jaubertie.

'That attitude wasn't necessarily typical, though,' he explains. 'Others in the area admired what I was trying to do, and would come and inspect our stainless-steel vats and considered our investment programme to be first-class. My attitude towards the French has always been very positive. I came to live in France, and I would never dream of sneering or jeering at a Frenchman. In fact, I have found the French to be amongst the most educated and cultured people in the world.'

And yet Château de la Jaubertie always remained an English haven, although by no means the last outpost of England in the Dordogne. Anne Ryman, more fluent in French than her husband, came to be more assimilated into the local community, a process assisted by her contact with the children and their schooling. To some English people looking at the Rymans from the outside, it was all rather confusing. This ambivalence was neatly summed up by a rather pompous Englishman who one day appeared at Jaubertie. After remarking how handsome he found the château and its environs, he sought to pin Nick down as to precisely how the proud *propriétaire* saw his identity.

'Do please tell me one thing, though,' he said, his tone a little haughty. 'I don't quite understand. Are you still English or are you now French?'

'I'm European,' Nick thundered. With Britain having only recently entered the Common Market, it was a retort which had the desired effect of stopping his interrogator dead in his tracks.

'We were certainly different,' Anne explains. 'And because of that we seemed to be able to get away with a lot of things. There was always less protocol with us and if we didn't follow some procedure correctly it was immediately brushed aside by the fact we were "*les anglais*". I used to go to the local markets regularly for shopping and I was continually meeting other mothers through the children. I enjoyed the integration, but I have to say that at first I really did miss my English girlfriends – ringing up someone and saying, "Can I come round for a coffee and a chat?" That's not quite the done thing in the Dordogne.'

For a person undertaking to relearn the fundamentals of French cuisine, Anne was making rapid progress indeed. Refusing to be restricted to one particular menu which she knew could always be relied upon to succeed, she would periodically transfer her allegiance from one favoured dish to another. She also soon saw to it that Percy the pig was not condemned to solitary confinement for any prolonged period of time, the château rapidly turning into the equivalent of a small self-sufficient farm, with sheep and hens and fruit and vegetables of all kinds being reared or grown within its grounds. Never happier than when at work in the large and spacious country kitchen of Jaubertie, she was constantly in the throes of making her own jams or preparing pâtés of every conceivable kind, and bottling and pickling whenever a spare moment presented itself. The net result of this supreme culinary effort was a standard of *gastronomie* difficult to surpass in the Dordogne or elsewhere.

With a constant stream of visitors to Jaubertie, Anne's cooking was regularly shared with those other than the immediate family. On one occasion two rather plump Americans from Florida's Palm Beach arrived at the château, the lady dressed in a bright-pink suit, with a perfectly colour-coordinated head of hair to match. The couple soon found themselves seated for lunch and being served *oeufs mollets* on a bed of lettuce and chives by way of an entrée, followed by stuffed loin of pork with fresh broad beans, the meal being rounded off with cake accompanied by plums which had been bottled in Armagnac. And every single item of that lunch was either Jaubertie-produced or home-made.

'You know,' the lady interjected, 'at home we tend to eat out of the icebox. But, gee, this is what I call *real* food.'

Nor was such heartfelt approval of Anne's culinary

talents restricted to the less discerning visitor from overseas. The French themselves, always eager to enter into a detailed discussion of any aspect of food, were frequently impressed, and it was clear from both the tone and substance of their comments that they had had only the very lowest of expectations concerning *la cuisine anglaise*. In fact Anne's small individual steak and kidney pies had a habit of being devoured almost immediately they were served, and all her dishes which hinted at India or deployed other flavours with which the French were not particularly familiar, proved to be equally popular and in demand. Nor, for that matter, were there any complaints concerning the typically French country cooking which she had learned, and improved upon, from Madame Ayral. Indeed, whatever type of meal she served, it was never long before a familiar round of murmuring and whispering began, with the unthinkable sometimes actually being articulated outright. *'Mais c'est extraordinaire qu'une anglaise cuisine mieux que nous!'* ('But it's extraordinary that an Englishwoman can cook better than us!')

Nor could numbers intimidate Madame Ryman. During her third year at Jaubertie it was suggested to her that the château might be an ideal venue for the meal which traditionally accompanied a rather chic annual tennis tournament in which she had become involved. 'And why not?' Anne had replied, never one to shirk a challenge. Immediately she began to think about what might constitute the most appropriate menu. Soon she had decided on an hors-d'oeuvre of *terrine de poisson*, a main course of *poulet au verjus avec haricots verts* and a home-made cheesecake baked with *fromage frais* for dessert, and it only remained for the hostess to be informed of how many she should expect to attend. When it was put to her that the most accurate estimate to date was 256, she did not panic in the slightest, and calmly set about baking, among other things, a further twenty-seven cheesecakes.

'They used to nickname me Madame Brouette – Mrs Wheelbarrow. Because I was always cleaning out the horses' stables and constantly pushing the wheelbarrow, often loaded with manure, around the grounds of Jaubertie. When Monsieur Bacco saw me doing this for the first time he was visibly shocked, and came running out calling, "Madame, Madame, you shouldn't be doing that – let me do it for you." Because I was the *châtelaine*, and it was quite clear that he thought that I should have been sitting quietly indoors doing my needlework. It was the same thing when he saw me driving the tractor. I shall never forget the look of horror on his face.'

Nick Ryman might not have been as sporty as his wife, who also managed to find time to teach aerobics and tap-dancing both locally and at a school of dance in Bergerac, but in his own way he was just as active and energetic. With his long-term programme of modernization and replanting well underway and Jaubertie finally beginning to produce respectable wines as a consequence, Nick turned his attention to the challenge of marketing his produce. The former financial and joint managing director of a large and successful English public company soon found himself turned into a self-employed sales representative promoting the produce of his own medium-sized vineyard in France.

To begin with, orders were few and far between. Then a Master of Wine, Serena Sutcliffe, introduced Nick to a mail-order firm which agreed to promote the wines of Château de la Jaubertie for a mere five per cent commission. It proved to be a highly successful venture, with 850 cases sold in the first year, 1,250 in the second and 1,750 in year three. But just when Nick was beginning to enthuse about the potential size of the

British market, the catalogue's buyer suddenly changed –
Jaubertie was out, another château in – which meant that
in year four not one case was sold in this way. Just as
well, then, that other customers would arrive
unexpectedly from time to time – Tom Johnson of High
Breck Vintners, near Headley in Hampshire, was one of
the first – to place the odd order. On one occasion a
German buyer from the firm of Ludwig von Kapf pulled
up outside the main gates of the château. After
announcing that he had only half an hour to spare, he
embarked on a lightning tour of the vineyards and *chais*,
and informed the owner that he was most impressed and
would be in touch in due course. He was as good as his
word, and in 1975 was responsible for placing the first
order for a full trailer load – some 1,200 cases of wine.

'It was a little strange for me becoming a rep,' admits
Nick. 'It was seeing things from the other side of the
fence. But getting orders for our wine was extremely
satisfying.'

Making a personal appearance in Britain, Nick soon
discovered, could certainly help matters along. But he
also learned that the process of selling wine could be an
extremely long, drawn-out affair, with a pattern of
trading which could hardly have been further removed

from the fast-moving world of self-service stationery. Rapidly acquainting himself with the rules of the wine trade, he knew never to uncork a bottle in front of a prospective purchaser – sometimes because the wine was destined to go before an official tasting committee, but often because the buyer himself would be unsure precisely which adjectives to use when describing the wine. Better to say nothing at all than to use a 'fat', 'round', 'full' or 'lean' inappropriately. For Nick, anxious to assess the size of the revenue he was likely to be able to count upon, this was a most frustrating aspect of the trade. A speedy verdict might be one delivered within two or three months. In fact a Norwegian company once sought to confirm an order for twenty-five cases of wine a full eighteen months after tasting, by which time not only had that vintage gone but the following year's too.

'I have to say that having been fairly well known in commerce – the Rymans name and all that – certainly did work to my advantage. Plus, in those days at least, I could charm some of the birds off the trees.'

But Nick also had a habit of sending some of them flying back up to their branches again. This was entirely attributable to his volatile personality. For although he was undoubtedly capable of showing great kindness and generosity, he also enjoyed a reputation for his rapid mood swings. While he did his best to conceal this side of his nature from people with whom he was involved in business, those in his employ sometimes found themselves confronted with these moods. Not that this distressed Joseph Bacco unduly. For it had not taken him too long to master the art of how to handle his new boss. The secret to success, he would later explain, was all in the timing.

'I remember one occasion when Monsieur Ryman was enjoying a glass or two, and I discovered a good technique: if you wanted to get him to agree to something you had to strike while he was feeling relaxed by the wine – because then you could almost be sure that the answer would be yes.'

As the years went by Nick's love for Jaubertie deepened, as did his wife's. 'I never go on holiday,' he had a habit of telling people. 'I am on holiday where I am.'

Yet there were many occasions when there was not much evidence of any holiday spirit. In one respect this was not of Nick's own making, in that apparently he could not help himself. For there were a number of basic do's and don'ts which he simply could not bear to see ignored – no matter where and no matter when. Being kept waiting was definitely one of his worst *bêtes noires*. On one occasion he was having his hair cut at a salon in Bergerac. He must have had a temper brewing because of the length of time he had been forced to sit patiently. For suddenly, with his head still wet from the rinse and shampoo, he leaped to his feet, removed the plastic sheet draped across him, shouted a number of unflattering remarks concerning how long he had been obliged to wait, and stormed out of the salon. It was no doubt all terribly un-English and impolite, but Monsieur Ryman was never again kept waiting *chez* Katlow.

This shortest of short fuses was often ignited by his son. A strict and uncommunicative father, Nick took it upon himself to ensure that Hugh should emerge as a well-dressed and well-disciplined young man. And woe betide the boy should he ever show the slightest sign of sloppiness in his speech or, still worse, ever complain of being bored. But there were two standards of discipline applied at Jaubertie: a harsh and inflexible regime designed for Hugh and an altogether more lenient set of rules for the girls.

'People would often ask in front of my father,' Corinne explains, 'if Hugh would one day come to work at Jaubertie. But Daddy would always point out that he didn't need anyone. He would often say he didn't know what he was going to do with him, telling him that he would have to go into the army for two years, and how that would do him a power of good. Hearing him run Hugh down all the time used to hurt me a great deal, and I found it most unfair.'

But Hugh was not the only boy living in fear of his father at Jaubertie. François Bacco did too. This was one reason, perhaps, why the two boys came to get on very well. To begin with it was François, two years younger than the *fils du patron*, who knew most about the local way of life – hardly surprising since he had been born and brought up in the valley of the Dordogne. He wasted no time in showing Hugh the ropes in and around Jaubertie – including how to start a tractor and manoeuvre it. Their friendship soon broadened to encompass most aspects of wildlife within the grounds of the château. Before long the two teenage boys were regularly catching birds together, felling sparrows, swallows, thrushes and blackbirds through the speed and accuracy of their aim with a catapult. Every now and then they would be spotted heading off together towards the tractor shed, where they knew several swallows were likely to be found, and as the birds would fly out in search of a safer spot the two boys would set upon them with their stones. They also had small traps to hand in which they would try to catch sparrows and thrushes, luring them with bits of baguette and occasionally roasting their prey. Considerably more respect, however, was shown towards the local pigeon population, both boys keeping their separate collections in a *pigeonnier* situated close to the pigsty at Jaubertie.

Since Joseph Bacco was a dedicated hunter himself, it was almost inevitable that the two teenagers would graduate to guns. To begin with, a small rifle with cartridges satisfied their requirements, but Hugh and François would occasionally sneak out together in an old *deux chevaux* armed with a twenty-four-bore shotgun. They would brace themselves to spot and shoot rabbits, although unlike their prowess at catapulting, their skill only ever led to the killing of two or three of the creatures. And if not shooting or fishing together, they would work side by side in the vineyards, removing stones from around the vines or, when the time was right, carry out some bottling in the *chais* – only to set off again together in the evening. Although they were from different countries and different cultures and were attending separate schools, it did not take too long before the two boys became the very best of friends.

While Agnès Bacco was certainly not in the same league as Madame Ryman in the arts of the kitchen, she could still produce some very tasty dishes indeed, including her speciality of tapioca soup *à la cervelle*, a concoction of brains and vegetables. Nor was her husband Joseph too shy to prepare the occasional meal, and he would from time to time invite both the Mondié and Ryman families for a *méchoui*, when he would assist in the roasting of a whole lamb on a spit over a large open fire. The mere fact that the Ryman children had had the pleasure of appreciating Joseph Bacco's cooking did not mean that he was automatically exempt from being an eminently suitable target for ridicule. And they soon discovered that there was seldom a better opportunity for them to enjoy themselves at his expense than when dark and threatening storm clouds would begin to gather in the skies above Jaubertie.

'I think I shall always remember Monsieur Bacco and his rockets,' explains Camilla. 'He would place them in plastic containers which he had cut up and filled with earth in order to provide some weight. Then he would light and send up four or five rockets just as the storm was beginning to break. But only for them to come straight back down again with a *phut*. He thought that they were going to go up into the clouds, separate them, and somehow prevent the storm. We would be peeing ourselves with laughter because we thought it was so funny. So whenever we would see any signs of a storm brewing we would all immediately seek permission to go and visit the Baccos.'

To Joseph Bacco, however, recently promoted to *chef de culture*, the idea of sending up rockets with a view to affecting the weather was no laughing matter. '*Vous allez voir*,' he would always insist, '*ça va marcher*' ('You'll see – it'll work'). In fact not only did they never do the trick, but he once almost inflicted terrible damage when a rogue rocket went flying sideways past the château and narrowly missed making a dramatic entrance through a bathroom window which had been left open despite the inclement weather.

While her children were laughing at Monsieur Bacco's touching faith, Anne Ryman was often worrying. She knew very well that there were still insufficient orders coming in. Anxious to find out whether or not the family's long-term future lay at Jaubertie, she took advantage of a trip to London to visit the premises of the Spiritualist Society in Belgravia. After paying her fee of

£5 for a single session, she enquired whether or not it was likely that the Ryman family would eventually be obliged to part with the property they had waited two years to acquire. The medium, a woman in her fifties, immediately made her prediction: the Rymans would not be parted from Jaubertie. Then, entering a trance, and without ever having visited their home in France, she began to speak of a grand country house and gave an uncannily accurate description of the entrance to the château, with its clipped hedges on the approach from the front gate, and the winding staircase inside.

'Wait a minute,' the medium said, just as Anne was preparing to leave. 'I can see something else. There is a ghost. I can see him quite clearly now, standing at the top of the stairs and smiling. He's got long and fair curly hair, and is dressed in a blue frock-coat and white breeches. His name is James and he considers the house to be his property which has simply been lent to you. But he is very happy for you to be there because you are nice and quiet, gentle people and because you are restoring his home.'

Anne did not know what to make of this information. But her daughter Camilla did. To her, not yet ten years old, Château de la Jaubertie became creepier than ever before. And yet her greatest fear was not an unexpected encounter with James – for she appeared able to accept her mother's assurances that he was a friendly spirit who wished no harm to befall the family – it was rather to leave the kitchen alone in order to go to the toilet after dinner at night.

'I was always afraid that someone would come up from the garden and look at me from behind the window. So I was offered various bribes and financial incentives to go to the loo on my own. Jaubertie just seemed to be so big and in the middle of nowhere. I used to be very scared, although actually nothing ever happened there at all.'

This was not altogether true. In fact Camilla was involved in the odd share of mischief herself, even if only in the lesser role as an accomplice in the aftermath of crime. For it was seventeen-year-old Hugh who had decided to take advantage of the absence of his parents one evening, slipping out of Jaubertie in his mother's brown Renault 4L and doing a reasonable imitation of a rally driver on the long and winding country road between Bouniagues and Labadie. His excursion was proceeding according to plan until the untimely appearance of a tree, which caused a most enormous dent upon impacting with Anne's car. With a year to go before being able to apply for his driving licence and with no insurance of any kind, Hugh beat a hasty retreat back to the château. Perspiring profusely and wondering what to do, on his return he immediately confessed all to both Corinne and Camilla. In the hope that they might be able to repair the bodywork themselves, the young Rymans set about the urgent task before them. Applying clothing to protect the paintwork, they began to hammer at the bonnet from a variety of angles in an attempt to restore the vehicle to its original shape.

It did not take them long to realize that their valiant efforts were doomed to failure and the three youngsters decided instead to sit down and hold an impromptu strategy meeting. Hugh's only hope, they concluded, was to lie. And the bigger and more elaborate the lie, the more effective it was likely to be. The following morning the children began to play out their carefully rehearsed roles.

'You can't imagine what happened last night,' Corinne began. 'You won't believe it. But some gypsies came to the house while you were out and they wanted to work for us in the *vendanges* as pickers.'

'We told them that that was impossible,' Hugh added. 'And that we really didn't need anyone. But they were so angry when they left that with their big caravan they backed up into the car. I think they did it deliberately, actually. Instead of stopping, though, and looking at the damage which they had caused, they just drove off and left. We couldn't believe it. We weren't sure what to do. I'm just wondering now if I shouldn't have called the police right away?'

'No,' Camilla chipped in, not wanting to be left out of the fun. 'They weren't at all happy when we told them that there would be no work for them at Jaubertie.'

Thanking their children for having acted responsibly and reassuring them that such an incident would be unlikely ever to recur, Nick and Anne accepted the facts as reported to them and never mentioned the matter again. The reason for their speedy endorsement of this entirely fictional version of events was partly that there were other, more pressing matters exercising their minds. It was not that the wines of Jaubertie were not beginning to do well. They were, for an impressive list of prizes and accolades had already begun to come their way, including a gold medal for an excellent Bergerac Rouge made from pure Merlot, a silver medal for their Bergerac Rosé and a bronze medal for their Bergerac Sec. In fact, between 1975 and 1979 Nick received no fewer than thirteen prizes from competitions and fairs held in Mâcon, Paris, Bordeaux and elsewhere.

Such honours were undoubtedly good for morale. The proud *patron* would immediately call in his workers to celebrate and give each of them a crate of wine. And Nick would then immediately move to distance himself from the applause, and point towards Henry Mondié instead. 'It's the wine-maker who deserves all of the credit,' he would always insist.

And yet none of those medals helped the till to ring at Jaubertie. Or if they did, they did not do so often enough. For now, some six years after his arrival in France, Nick realized that his finances were in a precarious state indeed.

'Running the vineyard proved to be incredibly expensive. Paying for the vintage, the ongoing permanent staff, new machinery to be bought, while ripping out the vines at the same time – I really had no idea how much it was all going to cost. My motto had been "let's forget all about finance and make the most fabulous wine". Crazy, I know. Until one day I suddenly woke up and realized that the whole lot had gone. And that I no longer had a single penny left in the world.'

BONDHOLDERS IN THE BATH

FOR A PERSON purporting to be on the brink of bankruptcy, Nick Ryman led a very glamorous lifestyle indeed. With the restoration of the château continuing apace, various VIPs and celebrities would look in from time to time at Jaubertie, where, at least once a week, a bottle of champagne would be opened and drunk, not in order to toast or mark a special occasion but simply for the extravagance of the act and the sheer pleasure of its taste. It hardly seemed to be a picture of deprivation and despair.

Driving around his extensive vineyards in a 1923 left-hand-drive Citroën Kegresse half-track, Nick looked and behaved more like the lord of the manor than a person heading for the Tribunal de Commerce, the French equivalent of the feared bankruptcy court in London's Carey Street. He had acquired this unusual vehicle some years earlier while negotiating the purchase of his last home in England, The Dye House. Having inspected the property, Nick had turned to the owner, a Mr Charrington of the oil firm of that name, and informed him that he had been most impressed, especially by the extensive gardens and grounds then maintained by three full-time gardeners. 'I have to say, though,' Nick had added, 'that the thing which intrigues me most of all is the two old wrecks which you have got outside under a tin shed.'

Charrington wasted no time in disabusing Nick of the notion that the vehicles referred to were fit only for the scrap yard. It was Citroëns such as these, he pointed out, which had earned their colours in a series of expeditions to Peking during the period between the wars. Then, turning to his butler, Charrington said, 'Bring George round to the front door, because I am sure that Mr Ryman would enjoy a drive in George.' The other vehicle, he explained, was named Mary. A car enthusiast since his teenage years, Nick later wasted no time in making contact with the estate agents, Knight, Frank and Rutley.

'I am prepared to proceed with the purchase of The Dye House,' he wrote, 'provided it includes both Mary and George.' This had rather intrigued the negotiator dealing with the sale of the property, and he immediately telephoned the Charringtons in the hope that they might be able to enlighten him.

'I think the price offered is one you should accept,' he advised. 'But Mr Ryman appears to be keen to have George and Mary thrown in. Before we take the matter any further, though, could you please tell me one thing – who on earth are George and Mary?'

Having restored Mary to her former glory and transported the handsome half-track to his château in the Dordogne, Nick would settle himself behind the steering wheel and slip into the role of unofficial guide, pointing out the Cabernet grapes on the left, the Merlot which he had planted on the right, and so on, with more than the odd anecdote thrown in. Cruising slowly around the vineyard at fifteen kilometres per hour, he soon had these excursions down to a fine art. It was a brand of PR that people tended not to forget, all part and parcel of the seduction of Jaubertie. Little did those visitors suspect that their tour leader had to think twice before filling the ample tank of his dark-blue Kegresse with the petrol it consumed so greedily. It was all a far cry from the day he had banked the Burton cheque which had instantly made him a multi-millionaire.

'It had been my intention to put some sort of nest egg aside,' Nick admits. 'But that idea soon went out of the window. I think I must have said to myself once a day, "Nick, you bloody idiot", because I had, as they say, blown the lot. I still wasn't regretting the whole thing, though. It just made me more determined than ever to succeed. I certainly had no intention of leaving Jaubertie in a hurry. Apart from which many people in England had confidently predicted that we would be coming back with our tails between our legs after a couple of years. And I know that more than a few of them would have rubbed their hands with glee to see us returning to the UK with our venture having ended in disaster. I certainly had no intention of giving anyone any such satisfaction, even though I no longer had two centimes to rub together. Apart from the asset of the château itself, I was broke. I was constantly worrying about how to pay the next bill and not at all sure what to do next.'

Hugh Ryman was not sure what to do either, although his worries were of an academic rather than financial nature. The only certainty in his life, it seemed, was that he harboured no ambition to work at Château de la Jaubertie. It was as well that this was the case, because throughout his teenage years he had heard his father say so many times that it had come to take on the air of a familiar if rather irritating refrain: there was little prospect of his services ever being required at Jaubertie. Apart from the occasional battering to his ego, this had never really distressed Hugh for the simple reason that ever since he was a young boy his ambition had been to one day earn his keep as a farmer, his love for the countryside having become even more intense since his arrival in the Dordogne. Electing to study for a *baccalauréat* highlighting literature rather than science, he continued to hope to pursue a career associated in some way with farming.

But growing up surrounded by the vineyards of Jaubertie, and often working in them during the *grandes vacances*, meant that for Hugh, if not for his sisters, it was almost inevitable that he should become involved in the world of wine-making. With the Rymans' lives inextricably bound up with wine, living at Jaubertie was rather like living above the shop, with no clear demarcation line between matters commercial and domestic. And he began to think that a more formal and academic training in wine-making might be appropriate. Convincing himself that oenology was a French form of farming anyway, he studied the syllabus of a much sought-after course at the University of Bordeaux. To gain admission, however, he first had to pass his 'bac D', although his school reports suggested that success was by no means to be taken for granted.

Henry Mondié, the oenologist at Jaubertie, could see the writing on the wall. While he had no particular bone to pick with Hugh in personal terms, he had nonetheless witnessed the growing interest of the *fils du patron* both in the vineyards and the various aspects of vinification. With Hugh quite open about his hope to one day enrol at the University of Bordeaux, Henry did not need anyone to tell him that at the château there would only ever be room for one full-time oenologist. And he began to feel distinctly ill at ease.

'I said to Monsieur Ryman,' Henry explains, 'that I quite understand that one day your son will want to come and take over the property, and that if this was indeed to be the case, then just to let me know. To which Monsieur Ryman would invariably reply, "No, my son mustn't work with me – we'll never be able to work together." Apart from which I could see for myself that father and son didn't get on. So in a sense I always used to receive the reassurance I was seeking.'

Although his background was firmly rooted in the Midi, Henry led a full and active life within the commune of Colombier, to the point where his voluntary activities had begun to take up a significant part of his spare time. Having purchased and restored an old house in the adjacent hamlet of Labadie, he soon proved himself to be one of the most energetic members of the small community, becoming a key player in the local Foyer Rural, whose self-imposed brief was to liven up the village through the organization of a series of *fêtes* and meals. So successful was Henry in his twin capacity of administrator and motivator that he was asked to chair that body, which enjoyed charitable status under French law. Never having shed the spirit of the boy scouts which had featured so heavily in his childhood in Cruzy, he had been delighted to accept the appointment.

While Henry Mondié was wondering how he might best serve the community, Nick Ryman was desperately trying to work out how he might be able to help himself. And there was seldom a more effective period of thinking time, the troubled wine-grower had found, than while soaking in a leisurely morning bath. Indeed it was while luxuriating in hot water that he suddenly hit upon an idea. He decided that, even though his seven-year stay in France had hardly worked out according to plan, he would attempt to repackage and represent his own damaged dream.

'I said to myself, "What does everybody want in life?" And I came to the conclusion that people often want either something for nothing or something exclusive – a status symbol like an expensive car or a yacht. Or, for many English people, I thought, to be able to say that they own a vineyard, or part of a vineyard, in France. I thought that I might be able to come up with a scheme which could give people the feeling of a proprietal interest in Jaubertie while offering them something tangible at the same time.'

Once out of the bath, however, Nick began to realize that his idea, however original and appealing, could easily lead to complications of all kinds. Initially he had thought that in return for a consideration he would let out the vineyard line by line of vines. So that a particular person could put up a brass plate and stake his or her claim to the tenancy of a few dozen vines. But that would have meant every individual who took up the scheme having to fill in a *déclaration de récolte*, testifying that harvesting had taken place, and, in theory at least, each line of vines being vinified separately. Determined not to be defeated by the bureaucrats or technicalities of any kind, he promptly modified his approach. The intention now was to try to find approximately 150 people prepared to make an advance purchase of ten cases of wine, which would be delivered free of charge to their door during the course of the following five years, in return for parting with £1,500. At the end of those five years, the theory went, the investor – or bondholder to use the jargon of the scheme – could opt either to receive wine for another five years for an agreed premium or be reimbursed by Ryman in precisely the same sum as had been invested in the first instance. The common objective behind these various proposals, of course, was to provide the wine-grower with the one thing he required above all else – cash.

Nick left for London to bounce his idea off a few people involved in finance. Having had the opportunity to think more about the small print of his proposals, he arranged to meet a stockbroker from the firm of Rowe and Pitman. The stockbroker appeared impressed and stated that he thought he would have no difficulty in finding a number of clients. But on one condition – so long as the project was underwritten by a bank.

'The bank guarantee,' Nick ventured to suggest, 'is my bright-blue eyes.'

The stockbroker looked more closely at the person sitting opposite him. He knew the name Ryman well. And yet it did not take him long to respond. 'They might be bright,' he replied, 'and they might be blue. But they are not going to satisfy me. You go and ask your bank for a banker's guarantee.'

Back in Bordeaux, Nick marched into the city's branch of Barclays. Much to his surprise the manager there indicated that supplying such a guarantee presented him with no difficulty at all, although he quickly added that he would require as security a charge on Jaubertie. Proud of himself for apparently having found a way out of his woes, Nick realized that his bondholder scheme had been born. Now all that was required was for it to be presented to the great British public.

'What could be more enjoyable than serving wine to your guests that has been grown, vinified, and personally bottled for you or your firm?' Nick's glossy brochure for bondholders asked. 'And what could be more effective and rewarding than for you or your firm to send clients or customers six bottles of your personal wine in a custom wood crate? You will also receive a handsome certificate and a twice-yearly newsletter describing the development of the current vintage. Plus as a certificate holder you are cordially invited to visit Château de la Jaubertie whenever you come to France. You will then be given a complete tour of the Château and vineyard and told all about the exacting methods of growing and vinification used to make this fine wine. Sign up now and look forward to proudly serving or giving gifts of your personal wine.'

It might well have been the familiar language of advertising hype. But forty-eight takers could hardly sign up quickly enough, thirty-three having come via the firm of Rowe and Pitman and fifteen from Nick's own brokers, Hoare Govett. That meant some £70,000 in the bank for the wine-grower. Which in turn meant that he could live to fight another day.

'The funds realized from this operation,' Nick explained in an accompanying press release, 'will be used not to buy a new Rolls Royce for *le patron* but to extend the vineyard, finish the replanting and continue the improvements to the *chais*. There remains a lifetime of work to be done.'

But financial battles were not the only ones being fought within the walls of Jaubertie. Because of his introverted nature and a tendency to seldom speak of his emotions, Camilla had grown up quite uncertain of her father's love.

'I was sure that my father wasn't fond of me as a child,' she explains. 'And that he didn't care for me at all. I was always scared of him. He would never take me on his lap or cuddle me. Nor was either parent often available to help with homework, Daddy because he couldn't speak French well enough – and Mummy because she was always cooking or entertaining. Running Jaubertie for her was like running a small hotel, with people coming and going all the time. Our only time together as a family was for meals. It was very difficult growing up having this permanent question mark over my father's love.'

In fact Nick doted on his daughter, 'Millie', whose angelic countenance often led him mistakenly to conclude that she could do no wrong. If only he had taken the trouble to demonstrate that love. But the *modus operandi* at Jaubertie was for no feeling of any kind ever to be articulated to any degree. Then at thirteen, Camilla began to suffer from anorexia nervosa, the so-called 'slimmer's disease' primarily associated with adolescent girls.

'I had no idea I had become so thin. My mother would scream at me; the more she would do so the less I would eat. Perhaps I was searching for my own identity, I don't know. Eventually I grew out of it. But my experience is that French families are much more into feelings and kiss-kiss. We weren't. We were so very English. Even our disputes would be relatively silent – just a raised eyebrow here, a disapproving glance there. And heaven forbid that you should ever talk about sex, another thing which the French seem to be considerably less hung up about.'

Nor was it all plain sailing with Corinne. The first in the family to show any sign of artistic talent, she had been encouraged by her parents from an early age to pursue her natural interest and ability in art, first by providing her with brushes and paints then, a little later, by paying for private lessons in water-colour technique after school on Saturday afternoons.

But Corinne also came to cross swords with her parents. The reason for this was that they made very clear their disapproval of a relationship in which she had become involved. Anne and Nick decided to send their middle child to boarding school in Bordeaux. But Corinne, fifteen years old and in love for the first time, still found it extremely difficult to cope with having her feelings dealt with in so cavalier a fashion.

'From that moment on I knew I was alone – that I had to live my life without my parents. Even sending me away did not break up that love. I was in Bordeaux, the other person in Bergerac, and we did the most crazy things to see one another. After a year or so I think my parents must have thought that it was all over, for they allowed me to have a studio of my own – which of course only made matters much easier for both of us. My relationship with my parents became very difficult because I would return to Jaubertie every weekend and pretend that everything was OK. Not that they ever challenged me about it. Because that was the way we did things at Jaubertie – you didn't actually speak about anything at all.'

Facing problems with all three of their teenage children, the Rymans were fortunate in being able to function effectively together as husband and wife. And nowhere was their ability to pull together in adversity more apparent than in their mutual determination to ride out the financial storms in which they had a habit of becoming embroiled. For if ever it happened to cross Nick's mind to give up the good fight, then Anne would immediately dismiss any such talk which might have led to their departure from Jaubertie. And should Nick happen to notice his wife's spirits flagging then it would be he who would bravely issue the rallying call for their survival and future success in France. It was only a matter of chance that their respective low moments happened rarely to coincide.

Anne was always only too willing to assist in generating income in any way she could. When it was suggested to her that Château de la Jaubertie might be an ideal stopping point for wine tours being organized in the Bergerac area, she immediately endorsed the idea of welcoming coachloads of parties twice a week. Here was the Ryman family at its best. Hugh would introduce himself and explain how things worked in the *chais* – 'doing the chat show', as they used to call it. Next Anne would lead off the delegation and serve one of her lavish three-course lunches in the usual way, and then, after plenty of singing, drinking and clicking of cameras, *le patron* himself would make an appearance and tell a little of the story behind the arrival of the Ryman family in France. Clutching a bottle of wine given to them as part of the package, the tourists would then head off again into the valley of the Dordogne, well satisfied with their three-hour stop-over at Jaubertie.

While the balance sheet could undoubtedly have been healthier, life at the château was anything but dull. Before the days of machine harvesting had come to Jaubertie an extremely tall and attractive English girl had applied and been accepted to work during the period of the *vendanges*. With her big blue eyes and curly fair hair, Mandy immediately caused great interest and excitement among the sizeable contingent of unattached male *vendangeurs*. Indeed a knife fight once broke out between two over-eager young men who had clearly become much more interested in picking Mandy for themselves than grapes for their employer.

But Mandy was about to discover that she had attributes other than her good looks. When she accompanied Anne on the drive into Bergerac to collect Camilla after her lesson in classical dance, the elderly and eccentric Yugoslavian directrice of the school of dance, Madame Desha, had taken one look at Mandy and immediately enquired of her whether she had ever danced. Yes, the English girl had replied, she had taken a few classes while growing up in Britain.

'Then follow me into the office,' Madame Desha continued, her tone brisk and matter-of-fact. And she promptly telephoned her old friend Madame Bluebell at

Le Lido de Paris, the famed night spot in the Avenue des Champs Élysées with a reputation for staging sumptuous spectacles, and suggested that she had an ideal candidate for her troupe. A few weeks and several rather rushed lessons later, and just as the harvest season was coming to a close, Mandy took a train to Paris to take part in an audition – to the regret of many a lovestruck *vendangeur* at Jaubertie. Madame Bluebell took little time before informing her that she could join her group of long-legged and scantily clad dancing girls should she so desire. With the sounds of Offenbach all around, Mandy seized the opportunity and was soon happily performing the high kicks of the cancan in the heart of the French capital, where she was to remain for the following two years.

Frivolity of this kind was quite at odds with Nick's often frosty manner. As the reputation of Jaubertie began to spread, with articles appearing from time to time in the British press, wine enthusiasts would sometimes take it upon themselves to pay a visit to the château. With a copy of the *Daily Telegraph* supplement tucked under their arm, they would confidently stroll down the drive. 'Saw the article,' the spokesman would announce, 'and just thought we would pop in and say hello.' If Nick happened to like the look of the delegation approaching he could be most welcoming and warm. 'Darling,' he would occasionally call out to Anne, 'that'll be three extra for lunch.' At other times, he understandably gave the intruders short shrift. 'I haven't asked you to come down the drive, have I? What do you think you are doing here? This is private property, you know. Would you please leave right away?'

Both family and friends sometimes suffered the same reception if they arrived at Jaubertie unexpectedly. With Nick Ryman one could never quite be sure when his temper would flare.

For a person such as François Bacco, however, who had spent all but nine months of his life at Jaubertie, danger was less likely to loom. He had come to know his father's irascible *patron* well. Always mindful of Joseph's motto that the key to success lay entirely in one's timing, François had good reason to learn how to choose his moments well. For he had not wavered in his hope of working alongside his father and becoming an employee at Jaubertie. Having completed four compulsory years at the local *collège*, he had gone on to learn a trade, qualifying as a metalworker. But throughout the period of his training he had dreaded the prospect of one day standing and soldering strips of sheet metal in a factory on an anonymous industrial estate on the outskirts of Bergerac. Having grown up in the healthy and open environment of the château, and with a love of the countryside in his bones, he longed to be able to remain there. Imagine his delight, then, when shortly before his eighteenth birthday he was taken on as an *ouvrier*, a manual worker, at Jaubertie. Pruning and cutting next to his father and breathing the fresh air out in the vineyards, he soon proved himself to be a most industrious and conscientious employee, in the best traditions of the Baccos, and with strength quite unexpected in one with so small and compact a frame. Anxious to learn the more technical aspects of wine-making from Henry Mondié, he was soon receiving instruction in the techniques of filtering, pressing, checking pumps, the cleaning and servicing of machinery, and many other aspects of work in the increasingly sophisticated *chais*.

As François was learning the practical side of wine-making, his friend Hugh was in Bordeaux at the Université d'Oenologie, which came under the auspices of the Faculté des Sciences, and where he immediately found himself swamped with textbooks on physics and maths. Having struggled with a literary *baccalauréat*, he had reason to ask himself on more than one occasion whether or not he had made a sensible choice in reverting to the sciences, especially when he was compelled to repeat the first year of the wine-making course. Just as well, then, that there were other compensations of student life. Foremost among these was an attractive dark-haired young woman named Anne Sophie Marie Vien-Graciet, whose ambition in life was to qualify as a doctor. They had met in a Bordeaux bar some time before the wine-making course had begun and their relationship had been rather slow in developing. And although Hugh soon became completely immersed in student life, it seemed as if the voice of his father followed him wherever he went and whatever he happened to do.

'About fifty per cent of the students were in a similar position to me – that is to say, with family interests such as vineyards behind them. But I never had it in mind that I would head straight off to work at Jaubertie upon qualifying – because I had heard it enough from my father that he didn't need anybody around. And yet at the same time he was encouraging me to become a wine-maker – I could tell that he was delighted that I had got a place on the course – so he seemed to be giving a mixed message. Nothing was ever said though – it was always ambiguous and vague. During the first year winemaking only accounted for a tiny part of the course. But as it increased I found it quite fascinating – the understanding and assessing of fine wines, especially after I had done a couple of training periods at premium places.'

Nick's message to his son might have been mixed, but the message received by most bondholders was certainly not. Their verdict was that the scheme offered good value, good service and, perhaps most important of all, good fun. Unbeknown to the owner of Jaubertie, many bondholders had apparently not been able to restrain themselves from bragging about the nature of their new and unusual investment. It seemed to represent one-upmanship that was difficult to surpass, and it soon became clear that talk of one's part ownership of a vineyard in the Dordogne had been working wonders at dinner parties in the stockbroker belt of Surrey and elsewhere. Without any advertising on Nick's part the number of bondholders began to creep up towards the one hundred mark – purely by word of mouth and personal recommendation. Every year in London, usually in or around June, a lunch would be given at the Hall of the Stationers' and Newspapermakers' Company – a flashback to Nick's previous incarnation – when the wine-grower would describe his latest plans for the development of his vineyards. And how he was envied by his bondholders as he stood up and spoke. Here was a man living out his dreams. It was probably as well for bondholders and *propriétaire* alike that this was all they saw.

'I had certainly expected to be going through much calmer waters after five years,' Nick admits. 'In fact I was still going through choppy seas and gale force winds after almost ten. It was only thanks to the scheme that I managed to get things back on to an even keel in terms of cash flow – by getting more and more members. But I only ever took on bondholders knowing that I would be able to pay them back if necessary. Fortunately the value of the château was increasing all the time, so they would always have got their money back, even if I would have ended up having to sweep the streets.'

It nearly came to that. Because, despite the increased revenue generated by the scheme, Nick's bankers were becoming ever more nervous. So nervous, in fact, that on several occasions they threatened him in no uncertain terms. 'Unless you can sort things out, Mr Ryman,' was the message, 'we are going to sell the château over your head within the next six months.'

But instead of concentrating on developing the assets already in his possession, Nick became convinced that the way out of his predicament would be to embark upon a period of sustained growth. After all, he reasoned, this was the formula which had proved to be the key to success during his years in the stationery business. And he always had it in mind that fifty hectares, rather than the twenty-seven he had initially acquired, constituted the correct size with which he would be able to first break even and eventually make a profit. Not only that: he also thought that in order to boost production it would be a good idea to take on some additional vines *en vrac*, in which his responsibility was limited to cropping the vines, making the wine and then paying the owner back. Impatient, impetuous and ignoring the advice of those financing his ventures, he began to buy up a number of adjoining plots in a rush to reach his magic figure of fifty hectares.

'The problem with debt,' Anne affirms, 'is that you are constantly running around trying to catch your tail. So when people look at our family photographs – like the one of the five of us in front of the château with Nick's half-track and surrounded by animals, they see only an idealized, romantic image of an English family in France. That's not to suggest that we didn't have our good times – of course we did. But there was also this most enormous stress, and I could see that it was beginning to take its toll on Nick. So if you could add a bubble to Nick and I on that photograph, you would have to write in the phrases really on our minds – "Are we ever going to be successful? Are we ever going to get out of debt?"'

Just as well then that Nick's motto was 'strive, strive, strive'. Not that he was the only one engaged in battle at that time. For on 25 April 1981 François Mitterrand emerged as the second strongest candidate in the French presidential elections, which entitled him to a place in the second round against the incumbent president, Valéry Giscard d'Estaing, scheduled to take place a fortnight later. Pursuing a strategy of making the Socialists the majority party of the left, while continuing to be allied to the Communists, Mitterrand went on to win a convincing victory in the play-off on 10 May with fifty-two per cent of the vote, prompting unprecedented scenes of jubilation in Paris and elsewhere, as his supporters celebrated the election of the first Socialist president of France since the founding of the Fifth Republic.

In Colombier, however, response to the prospect of Mitterrand taking power was much more restrained. Local people had never been particularly concerned with issues of *haute politique*, and in any event the politics that did emerge had traditionally tended to veer more towards the right than the left. Nevertheless, not long after the swearing-in of Mitterrand, it was the turn of the country folk of Colombier to vote again, this time to elect eleven members of the local municipal council, from whose ranks the mayor would in due course be selected.

'Having become president of the Foyer Rural,' Henry Mondié relates, 'I thought, why not participate still more in the life of the commune? So I decided to stand as a *conseiller municipal.* There were two lists of candidates, one from the left and one from the right. My political ideas not being terribly well known, both groups asked if I would like to appear on their list. I decided to go on the list being organized by Monsieur Revol, who owned a property situated next to Jaubertie, and which in fact at one time used to form part of it. I was one of seven people elected on the list of candidates of the right. Monsieur Revol was at the top of our list and therefore really ought to have gone on to become mayor. There was just one snag with that – much to everyone's surprise he wasn't elected. I didn't ask for my name to be put forward, but there seemed to be a general consensus that I was the most appropriate person, partly because of my work in the Foyer Rural, and partly because of what had been achieved at Jaubertie, where several new jobs had been created.'

Before taking the matter any further Henry thought that it would be wise to find out what would be the attitude of Monsieur Ryman towards the prospect of his employee doubling up as mayor. Having established that it was likely to involve only two hours of work each week, Nick immediately gave his blessing to the plan, aware that it could certainly do no harm to have a sympathetic person representing his interests in the town hall. And he relished the prospect of cutting through bureaucratic procedures of all kinds.

One week after the local elections the outgoing mayor, Monsieur Peyroux – who was looking forward to his retirement, having given many years of service to the commune – summoned the eleven newly elected councillors to the town hall. They now had to perform their constitutional duty and choose his successor. Having unlocked the front door of the *mairie* and settled everybody in, Monsieur Peyroux prepared to set off again without further ado. Before doing so, however, he handed his set of keys to Henry, aware that as the sole candidate from the majority group the oenologist of Jaubertie was the only person likely to be requiring them. An hour or so later Henry was proudly signing the minutes of that meeting and preparing some paperwork for the prefecture announcing what everybody apparently knew in advance, that from that moment on he was indeed *Monsieur le Maire*.

Unlike the inauguration of President Mitterrand, which had taken place in Paris amid the pomp and pageantry befitting a new head of state, the election of Henry Mondié as mayor of the commune of Colombier passed without the slightest trace of ceremony. However, this did not prevent the new mayor from promptly organizing a communal and in the event rather celebratory *repas campagnard* in the playground of the primary school at Labadie, a cold buffet to which the vast majority of people from the village were delighted to have been invited and able to attend. Sitting at the head table next to the *sous-préfet* of Bergerac, the guest of honour brought in to mark the importance of the occasion, Henry braced himself for his first official task – the presentation of a number of long-service awards, in addition to a special *médaille d'honneur* for the outgoing mayor, Monsieur Peyroux.

'I had never spoken in front of so many people before, and I was terribly nervous about it,' admits Henry. 'But once I got going it wasn't too bad. Unlike the majority of mayors I hadn't had the benefit of first being a municipal councillor, so I was a little worried about the various responsibilities involved. At the same time though I was enormously proud to have been elected, and honoured by the trust that people had chosen to place in me.'

Taking his seat again after a successful speech, Henry allowed himself a few moments to savour the applause. So many of those present seemed to be willing him to succeed. So many evidently endorsed his ideals. Sensing the surge of support for him, the new mayor remembered that in his jacket pocket he was carrying the keys to the front door of the *mairie* – two strips of steel which filled him with pride.

MONSIEUR LE MAIRE

THE MAYOR OF the commune of Colombier knew very well that he would not be wielding power on the same scale as his counterpart in nearby Bergerac, let alone those of the big cities of France. Indeed, since Colombier had a population of only 193, according to the latest official census, and since it was one of no fewer than twenty-one communes coming within the jurisdiction of the *canton* of Issigeac, it seems surprising in some respects that there is a *mairie* at all.

But it was in his rather drab base, a single-storey, two-room building which displayed the bright red, white and blue *tricolore* during *grandes fêtes*, that the new mayor would sit and prepare his campaign of continuing to bring the sleepy commune back to life again. With the tiny town hall open to the public for approximately three hours on Tuesday afternoons and Saturday mornings, and situated only a hundred metres or so from the Mondié family home, the thirty-four-year-old mayor needed no reminding that local eyes were now firmly fixed on him.

Henry did not disappoint. The art of being mayor, he soon discovered, was to know how to *monter un dossier* – to properly prepare and present funding applications for grants. For without financial assistance there was little prospect of anything ever being achieved. He thus spent a good deal of his time following the detailed procedures as laid down by the local *canton* at Issigeac, the regional council based in Bordeaux, or, occasionally, the relevant ministry in Paris. The guiding principle was simplicity itself – no *dossier*, no distribution of cash. Before long Henry had ensured that files and folders and projects and proposals were being dispatched to every single grant-awarding authority prepared to receive them. His efforts did not go unrewarded, for the commune of Colombier received a substantial allocation of funds for the maintenance of its roads, notably the section between Labadie and Ribagnac. The *salle des fêtes* likewise won a much-needed injection of capital – enough to pay for a substantial refurbishment.

Seven years earlier, when Henry had first come to the Dordogne, the local primary school had been perilously close to closure. This was not cost-cutting for the sake of it, but rather because of dwindling numbers, with only nine children registered at the school. But under his stewardship Colombier soon developed a reputation as a particularly dynamic commune, a role-model for others in the area.

'In the event other local schools came to us because our teachers proved to be very popular,' Henry explains. 'In fact we ended up with so many children that we had to ask for funding to carry out some building work necessary to open a second classroom. I think that eventually there must have been about forty children, and we managed to motivate many of their parents to come in on a voluntary basis and help out with whatever needed to be done.'

While Henry Mondié was expanding the facilities of his commune in the Dordogne, Hugh Ryman was expanding his horizons in Australia. After graduating as a wine-maker from the University of Bordeaux in 1983, he had been a little discouraged by the evident lack of enthusiasm for his services as a trainee *négociant*, a buyer of wine from the grower to sell to wholesalers or foreign importers. Having written to thirty different firms requesting apprenticeship work, he had received only three replies. This had prompted Nick to intervene on his son's behalf.

'I said to Hugh, "I am going to send you either to California or Australia. I'll give you a return ticket and some money in your pocket, and you can see what happens on the other side of the world." We happened to know Len Evans – Mr Wine Australia – because he had been to Jaubertie several times. So I phoned Len and asked him if he would be so kind as to look after Hugh – give him a good kick up the pants and not to spoil him at all.'

Aware that in the early 1980s Australia was the place to be as far as wine-making was concerned, Hugh packed his bags and prepared to set off for the Hunter Valley, where Len Evans, a Welshman-turned-Australian, owned the Rothbury Estate. But instead of being enthusiastic about the opportunity offered to him, Hugh did not seem to relish the prospect of departure at all. In fact even before he had arrived at the airport in France, he had not been able to hold back his tears.

'I don't know why he was so emotional,' his father admits. That's the complex character he is. Maybe he thought that I was dumping him in some way because I had said to him, "When you've learned the thing, come back." Anyway we didn't hear anything for six weeks, by which time his grandparents were practically hitting the roof. I told them not to worry, because bad news travels fast. Then we received a letter from Hugh saying, "This is the life", and complaining that he ought to have been sent away before.'

The handsome, twenty-four-year-old bilingual graduate of Bordeaux University was far from being street-wise, either in his adopted country or abroad. Travelling alone for the first time and armed only with a small map of the Australian wine industry, he had seen that the Hunter Valley was located some sixty miles north of Sydney and that it could be reached by rail. Struggling to understand the heavily accented English of the locals, and unable to control a series of mild panic attacks, he soon felt the tears welling up again.

Later, after Hugh had done a month or so of mainly physical work at the Rothbury Estate, Len Evans sought to point the young man in the right direction. There was only one place to learn about wine in Australia, he told him, and that was with Brian Croser at Petaluma, near Adelaide, the capital of the state of South Australia. After a little arm-twisting, Len managed to secure a place for his charge to work there. From Hugh's point of view it proved to be a move which was extremely worthwhile, for it was while at Petaluma that a most basic truth about wine-making finally struck home.

'It was only once there,' he explains, 'that I began to appreciate something fundamental. Even after attending university and having completed training courses at some of the top places in France, no one had ever bothered to explain to me that all wine is is a grape which has been processed. And that the flavours which are the wine, well, in actual fact it's all in the grape at the beginning.'

This moment of truth had been prompted by Hugh's having tasted grapes which were about to be crushed and comparing them with the red wine coming out of the fermenter. Only then had he been able to see the important correlation between the two.

'I understand your wine-making now,' Hugh said to his newfound mentor Brian Croser. 'All you have done is to retain the flavour of the fruit in the wine. And I can taste it in the grape too.'

The knack lay in keeping the fruit flavour both in the juice and the wine. If this was some sort of secret formula which Hugh Ryman had somehow stumbled upon, then Croser did not appear to be too distressed. 'You've hit the nail on the head,' he replied.

To the lay person looking in from the outside these new insights might appear to be little more than stating the obvious. Why, of course the flavour of the grape and taste of the wine are inextricably bound up with one another. And yet in France the attitude of winemakers has long been to stand back and commit themselves only once the wine is made. 'Le vin se fait,' they will insist – the wine will somehow make itself. That is why few French wine-makers will take the trouble to go out into the vineyards and actually taste the grapes with a view to assessing the quality of wine which is likely to emerge. For the prevailing philosophy in the motherland of wine-making is that once the juice has finished fermenting it is simply too young to taste. 'Il va attendre un petit peu,' wine-makers will state, explaining that it is necessary to allow for the passage of some time before one can properly assess a wine.

'To which I say "rubbish",' Hugh thunders. 'And yet I don't knock the classical training I received in any way.

Because at Croser's they would ask us foreigners questions and we would usually be able to come up with the right answers. So it was this synthesis of old and new techniques which I hoped might become quite a powerful combination.'

His thoughts having been revolutionized at Petaluma, Hugh became an instant convert to the cause and an ardent advocate of anything and everything which leads to concentration of fruit flavours – anti-vigour precautions, trellis management, low yields, canopy cover – in addition to a level of hygiene which would put many a medical practice to shame.

Shortly before her son had set off for Australia Anne Ryman had had her mind fixed firmly on the state of disrepair of Colombier's church, situated just a stone's throw from the main entrance to Jaubertie. With its base dating back to Roman times, and major rebuilding work having been carried out in both the thirteenth and fifteenth centuries, the church, which boasts an elevated position and a magnificent listed triple bell-tower, should, she felt, never have been allowed to enter into a period of decline. And she made up her mind to do what she could to reverse the process. Not that her motives were entirely altruistic. Hoping that her three children would one day be wed within its walls, she had no intention of welcoming worshippers into a place which was dark, damp and cluttered with nineteenth-century paraphernalia, as well as pictures and plastic flowers of all kinds.

Just as well, then, that Anne knew the right people. In fact not only was she on good terms with the one person in the commune with a reputation for getting things done – Henry Mondié – but *Monsieur le Maire* also happened to be her husband's employee. The Rymans were also friendly with a man by the name of Serge Royaux-Dehant, a renowned interior decorator who had made a reputation for himself through his restoration work at Versailles, once the principal residence of the kings of France and where the first scenes of the Revolution had been acted out. The mayor gave his backing to Anne's plan of allowing Royaux-Dehant to prepare some preliminary drawings, and summoned a council meeting in the ancient church itself.

It soon became clear that there was tremendous enthusiasm for Madame Ryman's initiative. Armed with sketches and statistics, she outlined what it was she had in mind, before going on to reveal that her son had been able to recruit well over a dozen volunteers to the cause, young people prepared to give a few weeks of their time during the summer holidays. Then another councillor intervened and stated that he worked with a local master mason, a Monsieur Berlugue, who could almost certainly be relied upon to provide scaffolding free of charge. Sensing the good will of all those concerned, the mayor thought that it would be appropriate for a formal body to be created to oversee the proposed work. And he suggested the name of Les Amis des Vieilles Pierres, the Friends of the Ancient Stones.

A few weeks later Hugh and his friends were hard at work removing mouldy plasterwork from the walls, sandblasting, restoring and renovating to the best of their abilities. Never shy to dirty her hands, Anne chiselled and scraped along with the rest, although she would usually absent herself after a couple of hours' labour so that she would have time to prepare a meal for the team of volunteers. Having rung the church bells in order to warn of their imminent arrival at Jaubertie, fifteen to twenty people would settle themselves down for a typically stylish Anne Ryman lunch.

The restoration of the church continued throughout the period of Hugh's absence in Australia. Every weekend approximately ten local people from the commune, the mayor included, would set off for the church in order to maintain the momentum of change. Seeing that it was creating a sense of civic pride and succeeding in bringing people together, Henry Mondié decided not to apply for financial assistance for every aspect of the work carried out. Altogether well over 1300 hours of labour were given free of charge, with at least twenty million centimes being saved through voluntary work. By October of the following year the project had been completed and a special mass was organized by Abbé Chaunac, the local parish priest, in order to celebrate the successful restoration of Colombier's little Roman church. To mark the importance of the occasion the choir from the Cathédrale St-Front de Périgueux was invited to participate, with a journalist from the regional newspaper *Sud-Ouest* sitting in and reporting on the proceedings.

'That day we were all dead proud of what we had done,' Anne recalls. 'We had managed to bring the church back to what it was, back to life again. It was done for the village, without anybody paying us a penny, and it was done with a great amount of happiness and laughter too.'

While Nick was unquestionably in favour of the project which his wife had been responsible for initiating, his own priorities continued to be more closely connected with the restoration of his own finances. But it had begun to cross his mind during this period, not unreasonably perhaps, that in the headlong rush to revitalize Colombier it was just possible that his wine-maker might have had reason to take his eye off Château de la Jaubertie.

'I had expected him to be giving his time as mayor free – just as my father had done for public services. I could see that the amount of time he was spending at the *mairie* was creeping up. I knew exactly what he was up to, mind you. He had made up his mind that he was going to be the best mayor in the Dordogne. And I can't say that I was terribly happy about it.'

Whatever his worries concerning the well-being of the vineyards, Nick Ryman rarely regretted his decision to uproot the family and settle in France. And as the years passed by, so the notion of returning to England became increasingly remote, almost slipping off the Rymans' agenda altogether. While the strain of juggling with figures and finances would on occasion drive Nick to distraction, the quality of life at Jaubertie was as addictive as it was unique. It might not have been doing wonders for Nick's heart, true enough, but it certainly ensured that the adrenal glands were kept hard at work, helping him cope with the constant stress. For at Jaubertie there was more often than not something exciting in the air. Indeed at around the time of the restoration of the church, this was true both literally and metaphorically, for the Rotary Club of Bergerac made contact to ask if a hot-air balloon could use the grounds of the château as a point of departure for an imminent lengthy journey. Of course it could, said Nick.

Then an American couple, Chuck and Rosie Tallman, approached Anne to see if she might be prepared to front a commercial venture they had in mind, in which both the name and photograph of the château would be used to promote select items of French *gastronomie*, with delicacies such as 'Perigord Goose Pleasures', 'The Foie Gras Duck' and 'Cocktail Onions and Capers' having been especially prepared and packaged so as to appeal to the US market. Not only was Anne happy to give her approval to this scheme, she was soon appearing in the accompanying literature as 'Madame de la Jaubertie'. And there was a further selection of French country jams, grape-seed oils, mustards, herbs, olives and honeys with which to whet the American appetite.

'We think this combination of French fare will tantalize the most discriminating gourmet's palate, as well as serve as a superb gift idea. We at Château de la Jaubertie are certain you will come back for more of this taste of adventure from France. *Bon appétit!*'

In fact not only did people in the Midwest of America, among others, not return for second helpings; they refused to sample these gastronomic delights at all, and the Tallmans' business rapidly folded.

There could be no stopping Madame de la Jaubertie's son, however. Thousands of miles away from family and friends, he was continuing to thrive.

'Australia was undoubtedly the most interesting part of my life – not only professionally but psychologically too. At the end of my stay at Petaluma I had two and a half months off. I spent one day and one night not knowing what I should do. It was the first time I had found myself in such a situation, having always been sheltered and protected until then. I decided to visit Australia and I hitchhiked around the country, stopping off to work on a cattle ranch for about six weeks, which was fantastic. That's why, afterwards, people said that I went off as a boy and came back a man, because after that I realized that I could cope, and that I never need panic again. I will always remember that day of wondering what I was going to do. It taught me that my future lay entirely in my own hands. And that seemed to give an enormous boost to my confidence.'

If only the same could have been said for the confidence of Henry Mondié. Unfortunately, despite his new and important position as mayor, his own self-esteem seemed to be proceeding in the opposite direction. He had come to feel that his position as oenologist was being undermined by a sudden and apparently uncontrollable outbreak of 'Ozziemania' at Jaubertie. And the root cause of his growing insecurity was undoubtedly the itinerant Hugh Ryman himself. For it was he who had returned to France in 1984 in the company of Martin Shaw, Brian Croser's chief wine-maker at Petaluma, just as the vintage was about to begin at Jaubertie. Aware of the importance of following protocol, Martin Shaw enquired of Nick whether or not it would be in order for him to comment on the methods of vinification used at the château. 'Of course,' the owner replied, eager as always to hear every point of view. The Australian then raced through a tutorial of techniques used in his country. The art of good harvesting, he argued, was to guard the grapes from exposure to air from the moment they are picked until the time they reach the bottle. That meant picking at night to begin with. Also essential was to have a man stand beside the driver on the automatic harvesting machine spraying the grapes from a watering can with a sulphur solution as they tumbled into the tank, again with a view to avoiding oxidation. Enjoying an instant rapport with the Australian, not one for half measures, Nick decided to give these innovative techniques a proper try, despite the fact that they were entirely untested in the Dordogne.

'So, on the first day of the vintage, I was faced with my French wine-maker and Martin Shaw,' he recalls. 'We had a very interesting half hour's conversation. I told Monsieur Mondié that we were going to be changing a few of our little habits. After the first morning, though, I said to Martin that there was no point in explaining at once all that we were going to do. We would have to feed him two ideas every morning, and two more every afternoon.'

Henry hardly had the time to take a stand on the relative merits of the changes taking place at Jaubertie, largely because they were being thrown at him so thick and fast. Shaw also sought to stress the importance of using an ultra-clear juice with which to ferment, and to do so at increasingly low temperatures, even below 15 °C, in order to freshen the taste. And all of this with the objective of retaining a full fruit flavour, just as had been impressed upon Hugh at Petaluma.

When Nick tasted the wines made from the 1984 vintage he knew right away that the quality of his whites was undoubtedly the best ever produced from his *terroir*. This was by no means a narrow or blinkered assessment, for *Wine* magazine agreed with him, and later voted the revolutionary wine as white wine of the year. And a number of other gold medals were awarded in Paris, Mâcon and elsewhere. It may have been Henry Mondié's injured pride which led him to be one of the lone voices of dissent, as he pronounced the award-winning wine *'fatigué'*.

It did not take long for the reputation of Château de la Jaubertie to soar. This was due in some measure to Esme Johnstone, a Harrow-educated chartered accountant who had founded Majestic Wine Warehouses in 1981 and who was in the throes of expanding his business at breakneck speed, just as Nick had done in the stationery business thirty years earlier. Nick had been introduced to Esme Johnstone as someone who made extremely good wine and who was keen to develop his share of the market in England.

'I went to Jaubertie, tasted the wine and thought it was fantastic,' Johnstone explains. 'It was selling for about twenty francs a bottle, which I considered to be way undervalued. We tried it at Majestic and it was an instant success. I think it's fair to say that Majestic established the English market for Jaubertie. We gave it plenty of PR – which Nick was superb at, going round our stores and talking to customers. Nick would buy the manager a bottle of champagne – that always went down well, automatically guaranteeing the future sales efforts of the person concerned. We became Jaubertie's biggest customer in the UK, although they continued to expand their market elsewhere.'

It was not just the sudden success of his white wines – which had by now come to be accepted as among the finest from the Bergerac area – that led Nick to participate so enthusiastically in the drinking of his own produce. For he had always enjoyed *un verre de bon vin blanc sec*, as he used to put it, long before he had come to settle in France. Nor would he seek to disguise his fondness for drinking the wines of Jaubertie. 'I am drinking the red reserve far too quickly,' he informed all bondholders in one of his regular and chatty updates on the latest developments at Jaubertie.

During the summer of 1985, however, one particular development took place which he chose not to write about in any of his mailings to the UK. Nick had continued to notice with irritation that increasing amounts of Henry Mondié's time were being diverted to his mayoral work. The situation came to a head as Henry Mondié was preparing to leave for his annual summer holidays in southern France. Because it was a particularly busy time at Jaubertie, with bottling and labelling going on, he informed his *patron* that should any particular problems crop up during his absence then he should not hesitate to make contact, and that it would probably not be too difficult for him to return to Jaubertie for a couple of days to sort things out if necessary. And the oenologist duly left the address and telephone number of where he would be.

'The day after my arrival on holiday,' Henry relates, 'I received a letter from Monsieur Ryman informing me that I had been made redundant and that my services would therefore no longer be required. After almost eleven years working together, I was completely shocked. What I can say is that it wasn't because of my work as mayor of Colombier because I would often make up the time by working late or on Saturdays. I returned right away. And then I saw what I had suspected for a long time – that he was getting rid of me so that he would be able to take on his son. That much was plain to see. I think that what I was most sore about was the brutal way that my years at Jaubertie came to an end. I think I would have felt differently had Monsieur Ryman come to me and said openly that he wanted to find a place for Hugh. But he chose to do things very differently.'

With his two daughters, Julie and Émilie, aged only eleven and seven, Henry felt he had good reason to feel sore. He was angry with Nick for the way he had been treated, and he was angry with himself for having believed his employer's former assurances that his future was secure. He claimed that on the basis of these assurances, he had turned down at least two offers of employment as an oenologist in his native Midi, and he kicked himself for having been so gullible and naive. Instead, the popular thirty-seven-year-old mayor, married and mortgaged like most men in the commune, suddenly found himself at a place he had not envisaged – on the dole.

A photograph by Corinne Ryman, showing a bottle of 1988 Château de la Jaubertie Bergerac Réserve.

(Corinne Ryman)

Inset: With his son Hugh away, carving out his own career in the wine business, Ryman was cultivating the skills of his young English trainee, Charles Martin.

(Nick Ryman)

Nick Ryman in his well-appointed study at Château de la Jaubertie, where he would often enjoy a glass of his own wine and a fine cigar.

(Nick Ryman)

Above: As Nick Ryman's success grew, so did the number of visitors to Jaubertie. Here he shows an overseas guest around the chais.

(Nick Ryman)

Left: Nick Ryman launches a Jaubertie wine for the exclusive Mirabelle restaurant in London's Mayfair.

(Nick Ryman)

Hugh and Anne Ryman, with two of their three children,
Eléonore and Maud.

It was Colombier's small Romanesque church that Hugh Ryman and Anne Vien-Graciet chose for their wedding on 27 August 1986.

(Henry Mondié)

Above: At various times the vineyards of Château de la Jaubertie saw Nick Ryman try his hand at growing Sauvignon Blanc, Sémillon, Chardonnay and Merlot grapes. His persistence paid off, for during the 1980s his wines received great acclaim, notably in France, where they won several awards, and in Britain, where sales soared. *(Nick Ryman)*

Right: After training in the wine trade in Bordeaux and abroad and then running his own company, Hugh Ryman teamed up with Esme Johnstone, the founder of Majestic Wine Warehouses to form the Rystone Group. After some twenty vintages, Nick Ryman decided in 1994 to sell Château de la Jaubertie to Rystone. For Hugh it was like a homecoming. *(Rystone Group)*

The handsome tiled well that stands in the corner of the vineyard, greeting visitors to Jaubertie.

Above: Camilla, the Rymans' younger daughter, holds hands with her father on her wedding day. Her earlier estrangement from him was over by the time of the wedding, which sealed their reconciliation.

(*Camilla Ryman-Chevalier*)

Right: Corinne Ryman, now a professional photographer, relaxes with a book. Hugh's sister was very happy that he had helped to retain the much loved château.

(*Corinne Ryman*)

FATHER AND SON

9

'I DON'T UNDERSTAND why Daddy wanted Hugh to work for him in the first place,' Corinne Ryman reflects. Having graduated from her *lycée* and gone on to study photography at a private college in Paris, she knew very well that father and son had only ever quarrelled and clashed. 'Because he never told him that he appreciated him in any way. Neither his work or personality. Nothing.'

His sister's analysis was entirely consistent with his own view of the world. Hugh's hope was to resume employment with Mestrezat, a Bordeaux-based *négociant* for whom he had worked for six months before returning for a second spell at Petaluma in Australia. Responsible for the handling of a number of *grands crus classés*, or vintage wines, Hugh had come to the conclusion that there was no reason why his future there should be anything other than bright. Then he heard of what had happened to Henry Mondié. And of how his father had chosen to pursue the path of making him redundant for economic reasons, which, under French law, meant that no other person could be employed in the same capacity for a minimum of one year. Not that Hugh was in a particular rush to start working alongside his father. On the contrary, he had spent the last few years attempting to ensure that their professional paths would not cross.

Henry Mondié's view of why he was made redundant is supported by Joseph Bacco, the Italian *chef de culture*. 'I was shocked when he got his marching orders, because we had worked together for many years. He hadn't neglected his work through being mayor at all. In fact the *mairie* was only open for a few hours each week.' Nick had, however, become convinced that Mondié was losing interest in the vineyard and was lacking enthusiasm for the new technologies being employed.

Whatever the case, Hugh had not been back from

Australia for long before he found himself working full-time as replacement wine-maker at Jaubertie. 'I would have preferred to have gone back to the *négociant* company in Bordeaux,' he admits. 'But my father expected me to work for him – and I felt it was an obligation. The vintage was only a couple of weeks away and I really didn't see how I could have refused.' Hugh Danvers Ryman – surely the most reluctant recruit ever to have been taken on in the history of wine-making at Château de la Jaubertie.

Nor were the rigours of French employment law particularly difficult to bypass, Hugh being rewarded for his services as a *travailleur indépendant* rather than appearing as a full-time employee on the Jaubertie payroll. Despite his manifest reservations about the wisdom of working with his father, his time there began promisingly enough. Charged with energy and enthusiasm from his second period of work experience at Petaluma, he began to build upon the many changes already introduced by Martin Shaw. The pattern of picking red and white grapes was no longer carried out solely on the basis of the traditional tests of the degree of sugar and acidity, but according to their fruit flavour. And Hugh soon demonstrated an exceptional ability to identify the precise moment of maximum flavour, simply by walking around the vineyard and chewing the raw grapes, a technique he had first seen employed in Australia. Pronouncing that one particular parcel of Sémillon might be ready, while an adjoining lot of Sauvignon was not, he made entirely subjective assessments which were nevertheless respected and rapidly proved themselves to be in the best commercial interests of the château.

There was considerably more to Hugh's philosophy of wine-making, however, than his unusual ability to accurately assess the fruit flavour of grapes. To begin with, the maxim 'Cleanliness is next to godliness' was heartily endorsed. And before the driver of the harvesting machine would be allowed within picking distance of even a single grape it would have been both meticulously serviced and cleaned. It was the same story in the *chais*, where every moving and non-moving part was cleaned repeatedly. Then came the approach of ensuring maximum skin contact. This meant that instead of the grapes being pressed immediately on arrival in the *chais*, they would first be pumped into a vat and left there for some six hours before being taken out and pressed.

And all the time one consistent aim was at the back of

Hugh's mind – the retention of full fruit flavour. These particular practices might not have been all of his own making, but he must certainly have been doing something right, for the rotation of Jaubertie's wines increased rapidly. Even the *grand patron* himself, not known for throwing out compliments or lavishing praise, let it be known that he was most impressed.

But Hugh's time at Jaubertie was not to be all sweetness and light. Far from it. 'Things started out quite well,' his father recalls. 'And there were times when he undoubtedly showed flashes of brilliance. I remember Martin Shaw making the point that Hugh was going to be very good because he always insisted on doing everything correctly – never cutting corners. But unfortunately he made one or two classic mistakes. I tried to tell him that. But he wouldn't hear of it – he can never accept that he has done anything wrong. I like to think that I can admit mistakes I have made. Not Hugh, though. I suppose that one thing we definitely do have in common is that we are both stubborn.'

'If there was a problem,' Hugh counters, 'it was always my fault. Then my father used to dictate the actual wine-making decisions. And this was compounded by never being able to sit down and talk things through. We soon ran into conflict over the running of a small family-run company – of who was meant to be doing what – with no clearly defined boundary between what was professional on the one hand and what was family on the other. I could never understand the strange relationship I had with my father. More often than not a talk would turn into a row. Maybe we are too alike, I don't know.'

The deteriorating relationship between father and son did not deter others from wanting to sample not just the extensive range of wines produced at the château, but the glittering lifestyle thought to be part and parcel of daily living at Jaubertie. It was a quality of life enticing enough to lure visiting dignitaries from all walks of life, including the former British Prime Minister Edward Heath, although his visit soon came to be remembered not for his incisive political comment or sparkling wit and repartee, only for the taking of a prolonged *sieste* after a suitably elegant lunch courtesy of Anne. The visit by the East Midlands Division of the Bentley Drivers' Club, however, proved to be a far happier occasion, as the owners of no fewer than twenty-three Bentleys pulled in for a glass or two of wine, having parked their handsome vehicles at the main entrance to the château, a watering-hole with appropriate panache, it was thought, during one leg of a major rally being staged through France.

Although the number of bondholders was continuing to rise steadily, thereby generating additional funds, other business propositions were considered on their merits. Thus when the French television company FR3 asked if the Rymans would be prepared to allow their home to be used as the setting for a six-part series entitled *Madame le Maire*, and offered an attractive facility fee in consideration of any inconvenience caused, it seemed too good an offer to refuse. For some six weeks Anne's catering talents were put to good use again, as the well-known actors Guy Tréjean and Marthe Mercadier, together with a first-class supporting cast, set about filming the antics of a lady mayor often at odds with her chef husband, as she became increasingly involved, often intimately, in the lives of various male members of the local community. It did not cross the producers' minds, of course, but they might have had a much more compelling programme filming the Rymans themselves, in whose lives there existed a good many elements to rival even the most addictive of soaps.

By the mid-1980s these had come to include marital

difficulties. Even before the departure of Henry Mondié, Anne had been spending an increasing amount of time in Bordeaux, the capital of the *département* of the Gironde, where, among other things, she had discovered the delights of real tennis. Played since medieval times and enjoyed by England's King Henry VIII, it is a sport whose rules call for an indoor court with irregularly sized walls and pear-shaped, lop-sided rackets. Despite its distinguished pedigree the game had come to be almost completely obscured by its descendant, lawn tennis, with the result that in France there remained only three centres, of which the court at Bordeaux was one.

'My wife was becoming more and more negative,' Nick relates. 'Nothing seemed to please her. She had got into a little group of women who were either divorced or living apart and I was quite sure that they wanted her to join the club. One day I had an agent for lunch and Anne was carrying on, saying how she was bored, that Jaubertie was too big and too this and too that. And he turned to her and said, "If you are unhappy here, you don't deserve to be happy anywhere." That soon put an end to that conversation.'

Camilla, the youngest of the three Ryman children, remembers the deteriorating situation at Jaubertie. 'One day my father called us together. He was completely fed up with the way Mummy had been acting – depressed, and constantly going off for hours walking around the vineyards and obviously so unhappy with her lot. I think it must have been a sort of mid-life crisis. Fortunately she pulled herself together and things began to pick up again at home.'

Witnessing the strains within his parents' marriage did not discourage Hugh from wishing to pursue matrimony himself, although he did take the trouble of attending a notary's office in Galgon in order to draw up a formal *contrat de mariage*. For on 27 August 1986 the twenty-five-year-old oenologist married Anne Sophie Marie Vien-Graciet, a student of medicine two years his junior, the girl whom he had met in a Bordeaux bar back in 1981 while supposedly studying for his *baccalauréat* in that city. And where else to be wed, of course, than the small Roman church in Colombier, which Hugh had helped to restore before his departure for Australia? And how else to arrive there than in his father's Citroën half-track?

Even before the service had got underway, the elderly priest was unable to prevent himself from launching into an impromptu eulogy about the many virtues of *la famille Ryman*, whose inspiration and vision had played such an important part in the renovation of the church. Unlike members of other monied families in the area, who had a habit of selecting a huge church in Bergerac in which to be wed, Hugh and his bride could think of nothing more appropriate than bringing the local church back to life again. Which, with 420 people attending, is precisely what they did. With the religious proceedings complete, the guests walked back towards the Rymans' home, forming a long and winding cortège, and preparing themselves to take an aperitif immediately upon arrival. Having had cocktails and canapés in front of the main entrance to the château, the French and English contingents alike were happy to leave the chill of the open air for the relative warmth and comfort of Jaubertie's two barns, which had been repainted and specially prepared for the occasion. Then, after a sit-down meal organized by outside caterers rather than the cordon-bleu mother of the groom, there was music and dancing, with fireworks lighting up the skies once darkness had fallen.

There were no complaints concerning either the quantity or the quality of the wine served on that most memorable of wedding days. But that did not prevent Nick, working with his newly wed son, from continuing to strive for improvement whenever and wherever such a possibility arose. Conscious that there can be no such thing as perfection when it comes to the making of wine, except perhaps as an abstract concept, the proud *propriétaire* of Jaubertie would nonetheless spend a good deal of his time attempting to approach it.

'There's only so much you can experiment with each year. And yet at the same time if you do stop experimenting and trying to better your product, you're dead. We would always give a lot of thought to the question of barrels, for example. You can get them from a number of different sources, Allier, Tronÿais, Nevers and eastern France. We tended to prefer Allier oak, because our vines are younger than those in the Médoc.'

In fact barrels can be different depending upon from where in the forest they have come, and where within the tree the staves have been cut. Then there are different barrel producers, different methods of seasoning and toasting, different thicknesses of wood. Aware of their importance in wine-making, Hugh suggested an experiment with the white wines of Jaubertie. He was anxious to acquire two separate *barriques* (hogsheads), one for some Sauvignon, the other for Sémillon. Not for ageing the wine, though, but to ferment it in.

'We started the fermentations in stainless-steel vats and then poured the fermenting wine into the new barrels,' Nick explains. 'After one month we tasted them and the Sémillon was spectacular. The Sauvignon was dull as I had expected and I suggested that we scrap it. But Hugh asked for one more month and I agreed. He did a few little tricks and then said, "Taste this now." It was sensational.'

There were also aspects of the relationship between father and son which were in the throes of becoming equally sensational, albeit for the wrong reasons. This situation was not altogether unrelated to Hugh's newly acquired status as a married man.

'When Hugh was working for me,' his father relates, 'he told me that he wanted to go and make wine elsewhere, as well as running Jaubertie. I said, "How are you going to fit it all in, won't it be very tiring for you, and how will Anne feel about her husband disappearing for three or four weeks at a time without coming home?" He didn't reply to those questions. Then when I suggested that he go away to do something, he turned round and said, "No, my wife wouldn't want that." So I thought, well, there you are. On the one hand he wants to do it, and then his wife is going to start creating and say no. His mother was also saying no to everything as well and continuing to be very negative. I could see that this was going to get us absolutely nowhere. I could see that I was always going to end up being wrong. And I could see that I was going to be left in the middle, being chewed up like a piece of string. I wasn't prepared to be manipulated by these two women, or anybody else for that matter. I have been through the army and I do know when I am being bullied and when I am being taken for a ride. And I thought it was about time that I put my foot down.'

At the moment when Nick was preparing to do just that, sales at Jaubertie were beginning to go up. Sainsbury's started to stock Jaubertie's Sauvignon Blanc; negotiations with Marks & Spencer were well underway with a view to having a Jaubertie wine appear on their shelves. And the critics themselves, people who can make or break reputations in the world of wine, could hardly pen paragraphs of praise quickly enough. According to *Harpers* magazine Nicholas Ryman was 'the man who had put class into Bergerac'. At the same time Jane MacQuitty was enthusing in *The Times* about the château's '86 Bergerac Sec: 'I loved its fresh, elegant, elderflower and gooseberry-like scent and taste –

perfect as a spring *apéritif* or with fish.' And writing in the rather pretentious language favoured by some critics, Jill Goolden chose to applaud Jaubertie's Rosé in the *Mail on Sunday*'s *YOU* magazine, although in a style entirely her own.

'It is magically coloured like a limpid strawberry lollipop,' she wrote. 'But don't get me wrong, it's certainly no sweet *bonbon* of a wine. The haunting scents of violets and rose petals are captured, with that unmistakable whiff of cake you find in cabernet-based rosés. It's thrillingly young wine, of course, as good rosés should be, and boasts a frivolous fresh fruitiness, teasing you to believe there might be a hint of sweetness. Dive into the glass, though, and you'll find the sweetness is just an attractive pretence; the wine is actually thoroughly grown up and dry. If I were to spy it on the dinner table, my hopes for the evening would certainly soar.'

With such glowing tributes regularly appearing in the English press and business beginning to boom, it was not surprising that Nick's hopes also soared sky high. Instead of taking the view that fifty hectares of vineyard was the correct size, he started to think in terms of cropping three times that amount, with the possibility of producing anything up to 100,000 cases of wine. Thus when a young Englishman called Charles Martin wrote to him to ask if there might be the possibility of employment during the '87 vintage, Nick replied right away that of course there was room for another pair of hands at Jaubertie. Like the *patron* himself, Martin had come to wine-making by a roundabout route, having graduated from Plumpton Agricultural College in East Sussex before going on to work in the contract milking business. It was only when an exchange programme had taken him to university in Minnesota, and from there to California for the vintage, that he had caught the wine bug. A gregarious character whose enthusiasm and deep, raucous laugh are equally contagious, he had also acquired experience both in Australia and New Zealand. And it was while working in the south Pacific that he had first come to hear of Nick Ryman when browsing through a trade magazine.

'I was pining for a bit of European culture. You know, an old house, an avenue of trees. And I was excited at the idea of making wine in France. I was in Hong Kong at the time, travelling about a bit, when I phoned my mother in England. She said, "Come back, you've got a job at Château de la Jaubertie." It was just for the harvest period, mind you, beginning in the September of 1987.'

He had no way of knowing it, of course, but by the time Charles Martin arrived in the Dordogne to take up his temporary employment at Jaubertie, he was walking into a bloody battlefield. For the relationship between father and son had deteriorated to such an extent that they were able to communicate with each other only by exchanging notes. And even in these written messages they were unable to agree. Forbidden by his father from having his meals in the château, Hugh could occasionally be glimpsed looking dejected as he ate alone at the restaurant of the Hôtel des Voyageurs in nearby Bouniagues, the place where Henry Mondié had found lodgings thirteen years earlier. And although Hugh's home continued to be in Bordeaux – another of very many bones of contention – when he slept at Jaubertie he would invariably do so not in the bedroom in which he had spent the greater part of his teenage years, but in the inhospitable and distinctly pungent surroundings of the *chais*. Not because of any ardent desire on his part to become more closely involved with his work, but for the simple reason that he was under a paternal order banning him from entering the main building of the château itself.

Being caught up in the increasingly bitter battle between her husband and son was difficult enough to endure. But for Anne Ryman it was the contrast with the red-carpet treatment being accorded Charles Martin which would prove to be still harder to accept.

'When I first arrived at Jaubertie Nick and Hugh had already fallen out,' Martin affirms. 'The whole situation was very sad – although not of my making, I might add. The thing about Nick is that he either loves you or hates you. I guess I must have come into the first category, although I realized fairly early on that it would be much more sensible to get things on to more of a business footing. But Nick continued to treat me like a long-lost son.'

For Anne, however, Charles Martin was anything but troublefree. On the contrary, the fuss that her husband was making of the new *stagiaire* (trainee) was not only totally incomprehensible but utterly repugnant to observe, to the point of coming close to driving her away from Jaubertie. 'In the end Charles Martin moved in with us,' Anne explains. 'And I was the one who had to look after him. He was being wined and dined with all the best château wines and all the rest of it. I was even told that Charles Martin was the future of Jaubertie. And there was my own son travelling backwards and forwards to Bordeaux, or sleeping in the *chais*. Well, I'm sorry, but I dug my heels in and said that I was just not prepared to put up with it.'

The mere fact that his personal life was disintegrating before his very eyes did not distract Nick from pursuing his ambitious projects for the expansion and development of Jaubertie. In fact he appeared to throw himself into his work with renewed vim and vigour. And despite the turmoil all around, the '87 vintage – the fifteenth since his arrival in France – began smoothly enough and entirely according to plan. Since he had already installed an enormous new compressor, a juice chiller and seven more large stainless-steel tanks, the vintage was handled at a much greater speed than during previous years.

With his wines being drunk in Japan, Germany and America, in addition to featuring in many English supermarkets, off-licences and other retail outlets, Nick became more and more convinced that he really ought to be finding or buying two and a half to three times more vines than the fifty hectares which had just been cropped. And with that in mind he began to think about the possibility of moving the *chais* to a different part of

Jaubertie or, failing that, to significantly extend and improve the existing site. Architects were contacted, costings calculated and bold new plans drawn up accordingly.

Having demonstrated what could be done with white wines, Nick turned his attention to his reds. The problem at Jaubertie had always been one of lack of colour, mainly because the previous owner, Robert Sauvat, had planted large quantities of Merlot, with a very low density of vines per hectare. Determined to rid Bergerac of its long-standing identity problem whereby its reds were frequently considered to be but a poor man's Bordeaux, Nick gave instructions to cut through the roots of the relevant vines with a long knife, a technique which appeared to improve their colour out of all recognition. Again the critics wasted no time in rallying to the cause. 'Close your eyes,' John Bond wrote in *The Grapevine*, 'and you could be in the Hunter Valley drinking fine Australian red wine, except that this Bergerac also possesses some of the finesse of Bordeaux.'

As the winter of 1987 approached it was time for Nick to think about preparing the second of his twice-yearly mailings to the growing band of bondholders in England. 'This year,' he informed them in a letter headed

'Singing in the Rain' on account of the recent bout of wet weather, 'was the last where the wines were made by my son, Hugh, who is now moving on. During this vintage I have had the assistance of Charles Martin in the *chais* and he will now take over the responsibility of making the wine together with me. I have every confidence that together we shall make better and better wines. You will have the chance to meet Charles either here or in England at the tasting or at the luncheon planned for next May.'

Nick clearly had no intention of inflicting his bondholders with a graphic account of Hugh's departure from Jaubertie. But his paragraph was nonetheless a little economical with the truth. Hugh was indeed moving on – for the simple reason that the period of his employment had been terminated by his father.

'All I ever wanted to do during my time there,' Hugh relates, 'was to get things on to an even keel financially. I had grown up in that property. I felt I had helped to save it from bankruptcy. I even remember attending one meeting with my father and two bankers and their saying quite clearly, "Why don't you sell the château and move elsewhere?" Somehow we had managed to get through all of that. And I think it's fair to say that it was the introduction of Australian techniques which was responsible for things really taking off at Jaubertie. But we had never communicated in the past – not even a little – so how on earth was it ever going to happen in business? And in the middle of all this things were rather unpleasant between my parents, which upset me a great deal. I think that the last day I spent at Jaubertie was one of the saddest days of my life.'

Preparing to leave Jaubertie for the last time, Hugh turned to his father. Despite the many months of acrimony between them, he sought to express his gratitude for having been given the chance to work at the chateau.

'Yes,' Nick said. 'You destroyed one of the best opportunities you ever had in your life. I'm afraid that you just didn't have the guts to make it work for you.'

Hugh was not in the habit of answering back, least of all to his parents. He had been brought up to do otherwise. On this occasion, however, he decided to break with tradition.

'One day,' he informed his father, 'I'll show you the guts I have.' And with those words he drove away from Jaubertie.

IN SEARCH OF THAT SWEET TASTE

SHORTLY BEFORE CHRISTMAS 1987 Nick travelled from Bergerac to Buckinghamshire. He had been invited to celebrate the sixtieth birthday of Clive Aston, an old friend who for many years had accepted the additional responsibility of being a trustee to the three Ryman children. It was also an ideal opportunity for Nick to visit Desmond, his brother and former business partner, and his wife Cicely, since they lived only half a mile or so away.

But Nick was not much in the party spirit that weekend, as his sister-in-law recalls. 'I remember saying to Desmond, "You know, Nick looks so ill." He seemed to be very run down. And just as he was preparing to leave before returning to France I could see that he was almost crying as he went out through the front door.'

Perhaps this foreshadowed more troubled times to come, because by the time Nick arrived back in Bordeaux there was no shortage of subjects over which the tears could flow. For the woman with whom he had fallen in love at first sight almost thirty years earlier, the woman who had steadfastly battled by his side and done more than her fair share to ensure the success of Jaubertie, had decided that the time had come for them to go their separate ways.

'Previously I had just put a brave face on it all,' she explains. 'Then suddenly, with everything that had happened to Hugh, it all went bang. I think that many of us spend our lives looking for the pot of gold at the end of the rainbow, and then when you get there, you realize that that's not what life is all about. From that summer on I had also been very tired, having had lots of guests at the château. Then there had been an awful row between Nick and my parents. Eventually I couldn't bottle things up any more and everything exploded within me. Despite that, it was still a considerable wrench to leave because I love Jaubertie.'

But not the man whose dream had been to buy a vineyard and make the finest wines ever produced in the Bergerac area. His marriage was in tatters and the younger generation of Rymans were not there to rally round and offer support. Nick and Hugh were no longer on speaking terms, and looked likely to remain locked in silent conflict for some time, since the concepts of flexibility and forgiveness did not come easily to either man. Camilla was preparing a master's degree in international business studies at the University of Paris III, linked administratively to the Sorbonne, the historic seat of learning founded back in the middle of the thirteenth century. And Corinne was likewise in the capital, cleverly combining creativity and commerce through her work as a professional photographer.

Yet the seductive setting of Jaubertie continued to dazzle almost all who arrived there, including a number of journalists, many of whom seemed reluctant to seek out material which might result in the shattering of their own illusions, let alone those of their readers. 'Nick Ryman is a happy man,' Sheila Keating declared in the *Sunday Express* magazine, 'as he sinks deep into his dining chair and raises an ample glass of the rich, mulberry-coloured wine he has saved until the end of a fine lunch of *cassoulet*, strawberries and Bavarian cheese.' In fact it was Camilla, always closest to her father, who was the first family member to return to the château. And there she found not a man basking in happiness, as frequently depicted in the press, but one perilously close to the edge of despair.

'I arrived one evening and found my father crying. Daddy was in a very bad way, close to breaking down altogether. We would start to talk, whereupon he would just begin crying again. I was on his side one hundred per cent. Mummy had left in a very abrupt and brutal fashion. It was the way she went about it which I found difficult to accept. She didn't have the courage to stand up and say, "I'm leaving because I am unhappy." She said, "I'm leaving because of the way you are treating Hugh." And it was strange to see my father – who had shown so little emotion in his life – suddenly shedding tears in front of me. Because Daddy's way of loving, and therefore many of our intimate moments, had been by having a glass of wine together – a kind of code, I suppose – rather than through expressing any feeling outright. That made it difficult for me to show emotion too, and to say the words which were really on my mind – "I love you."'

Despite the lugubrious atmosphere hanging over Jaubertie, Camilla – who since her teenage years had dispensed with the French version of her name – was excited at the prospect of seeing Knocky, Perry and Tiger, the three horses which had accompanied the Rymans on their arrival in France thirteen years earlier. For it was riding, together with ballet, which had featured so heavily in her childhood, taking up the greater part of her free time. She was about to set off for an adjoining field to find them when her father informed her, 'I'm sorry, but there are no more horses.' Nick sought to explain to Camilla that since it had always been her mother who had taken care of them, he had been left with no alternative but to give them away.

'I was shocked to hear that the horses had gone,' Camilla recalls. 'Knocky was mine, the horse I had grown up with. So for me that sad news represented the end of many things. The end of the marriage. The end of my childhood. When your parents split up when you are twenty years old, you can't help but say to yourself, "My God, there must have been so many things which I simply didn't see."'

There were a number of other things too which she could now see – one of them all too clearly. Her father appeared to have become totally committed to Charles Martin, who, within a matter of months, seemed to have metamorphosed from seasonal worker and *stagiaire* into the darling of Jaubertie.

'Give five wine-makers similar lots of grapes,' Nick would often tell visitors to the *chais*, 'and they will make five entirely different wines. The job of *le patron is* to find the right person and then to tell him the type and style of wine you want to make. To me the wine-maker is the most important person in the world.'

And he certainly treated his young wine-maker as such, to the point of considering a possible restructuring of his company in France so as to enter into a formal partnership agreement with his new employee. With such an enticing and potentially valuable carrot being dangled in front of him, Martin responded as one might expect, with a total commitment to the interests of Jaubertie as well as his own. Allowed a long rein by his paymaster and principal fan, he set about doing what he could to improve the running of the vineyard, redoubling his efforts on learning that his entire future might well be bound up there. Unlike some wine-makers, who consider the key to success to lie almost exclusively in the *chais*, Martin held that the vineyard mattered above all else. Building upon his background in agriculture, his philosophy was to achieve high standards at the pre-fermentation stage, so that the likelihood of having to add anything to the wine later on would be reduced. As well as introducing a new type of trellis and using the vine canopies in an innovative way, he also launched an extensive programme of grassing between the rows of vines, the theory being that the grass would absorb the moisture from the surface cap of clay, thereby sending the roots of the vines deeper into the soil. His hope was that the more interesting minerals and vitamins in the limestone below would be found and absorbed, which in turn would strengthen the vines, improve the flavour of their fruit and in due course pave the way for the making of more complex wines.

'The vineyard is looking better than ever thanks to Charles,' Nick informed his bondholders in another of his regular newsletters. 'We continue to grass down between the rows and have now decided on the ideal variety. We are more and more convinced that this method of viticulture will improve the quality of the grapes.' And unlike other updates, which for the previous decade Nick had signed alone, this particular communication closed 'with kind regards from

Charles and myself'. Charles Martin, it seemed, could do no wrong.

The sun was not shining so brightly for Hugh Ryman. Having decided to set up his own small *négociant* business, named HDR Wines after his initials, he was in the process of being turned down point-blank by a dozen different banks. The reason for the distinct lack of interest in his application for funds was quite simple: he was in no position to provide the banks with the collateral they required. And for a while it looked as though his ambitious projects to make wine in the south-west of France, notably in Gascony, Limoux and Duras, would not get off the ground at all. Then the Banque Nationale de Paris appeared to offer a glimmer of hope. Provided the twenty-seven-year-old oenologist could produce two pieces of paper, he was informed, these would be sufficient to meet the bank's requirements and therefore his plans could proceed. The first was a letter from a person prepared to act as guarantor; the second, proof from a prospective purchaser that there was indeed likely to be a market for the light, easy-drinking wines he was promising to create.

Unable to turn to his own family, Hugh approached his father-in-law, Pierre Vien-Graciet, and asked if he would be willing to throw a financial lifeline to HDR Wines should the situation require it. Encouraged by a positive response, he immediately telephoned Rodney Kearns, the purchasing director of Majestic Wine Warehouses. Explaining that it was his intention to purchase and vinify other people's crops, he enquired whether or not Majestic would agree to sign a letter in which a pledge would be given to buy the wine he was hoping to make – even though Kearns had clearly not had the opportunity of tasting it and was not likely to for some time. Hugh had already consulted company chief Esme Johnstone, who knew him well from his earlier incarnation at Jaubertie, and an affirmative answer was again forthcoming.

It was as well for Hugh that his wife, Anne, was able to supplement her basic salary by working overtime. Based at the Hôpital St-André in Bordeaux, where she was coming towards the end of her seven-year course in medicine, she made a financial contribution which helped considerably to relieve the pressure on the couple as Hugh set about launching his fledgling business. Also helpful was the fact that Anne's father had previously purchased a flat in the centre of Bordeaux, so that there were no monthly mortgage payments to worry about. Not that this encouraged Hugh to rush out and rent a plush suite of offices on the Esplanade des Quinquonces, where emerald statues glisten in spray from the marble fountains, the hub around which the world of French wine has revolved for generations. Preferring to keep his overheads to a minimum, he chose to do all the paperwork in a tiny room at home. Although the owner of neither a winery nor a vineyard, Hugh was finally ready to set about the business of making wine – Australian-style, of course – and to do much of the physical work of vinification himself. He had in mind preparing a Sauvignon in Duras, a Chardonnay at Limoux, a town situated to the south of Carcassonne in Languedoc-Roussillon, in addition to a Vin de Pays des Côtes de Gascogne.

'I was happy to be doing my own thing, but a little bitter about what had happened. I was definitely motivated by showing my father what I could do – but to prove something to myself at the same time. I also learned from Esme Johnstone about the importance of turning into a good PR machine, and of the need for your wines to be talked about. Mind you, I think I would have had enough wine to drink for a lifetime if things had gone wrong.'

But they did not. In 1988, his first year in business alone, Hugh produced 18,000 cases of wine, with his Ugni blanc Gascogne and wood-aged Chardonnay both emerging as instant successes. In fact all three wines, including the Sauvignon – produced, to local disbelief, next to a pigsty – displayed an aromatic, fruity character unfamiliar in the average bottle of 'cheap 'n' cheerful' dry white. The style was in the same fashionable vein as New World wines, but at half the price. No wonder the multiples soon began to queue up to acquire any case of wine stamped with the initials HDR – the promise, it seemed, of a clean and fruity wine at an excellent price. As for HDR himself, 1988 was a flying start which had exceeded all expectations, with the promise of still greater things to come.

'I was friendly with both father and son,' Esme Johnstone explains. 'The range of wines produced at Jaubertie was by definition limited – whereas Hugh's wines were not. So we began to buy from Nick and Hugh at the same time. But the fact that we dealt with them both did not constitute a conflict of interest in any way.'

That was certainly not the way things were viewed at Jaubertie, as Charles Martin is quick to point out. 'As soon as Hugh left he became competition to us. He went to see our first major customer in the UK – Majestic Wine – and I know that to a certain extent we lost customers because Hugh was going to them, with good-quality wines, either through a consultancy or partnership agreement. He was doing that very successfully and biting into our market. And what was motivating him one hundred per cent was knowing that he was putting the boot into his dad as he went about it.'

The more alienated Hugh became from his father, the more thoroughly Martin was groomed as heir-apparent to the château. Acting on his earlier idea of entering into a partnership agreement with Martin, Nick now altered the legal framework of Jaubertie so as to allow for a fifty per cent share of a holding company to be held by his English lieutenant.

He might not have been speaking to his father, but that did not prevent Hugh from frequently hearing from him, albeit in a series of messages which must have become lodged in his subconscious mind years before their painful parting of the ways. In fact Nick's oft-cited slogan, 'You have always got to be the best, otherwise it's not worth doing at all', was not only heartily endorsed by his son but adopted and acted on as if it was his own.

PAINTING BY STEFAN KNAPP

CHATEAU DE LA JAUBERTIE
1989
BERGERAC SEC
APPELLATION BERGERAC SEC CONTRÔLÉE
HENRY RYMAN S.A.
COLOMBIER DORDOGNE
12,5% vol.   PRODUCE OF FRANCE   75 cl.℮

Among the various successes of Jaubertie has been its dry white Bergerac.

Nor did not speaking to his father hinder Hugh from finding out precisely what was happening at the château. When he heard of the restructuring due to take place at Jaubertie he immediately sent off a fax in which, with a touch of irony and plenty of anger, he informed his father that as the owner of one share in the company he wished formally to place his disapproval on record.

'I didn't mind being disinherited,' Hugh insists, 'because I never expected anything. But I did object to assets going to an outsider – in the full knowledge that my father had never been treated in that way. On the contrary, he had had the family business handed to him on a platter while still in his early twenties. I really couldn't understand what he was up to at all.'

It was this feeling of outrage and injustice which made Hugh determined that the château should not be allowed to slip from the Ryman family's control quite so easily. At least not without a fight. Having only recently started his own business, he was not in a particularly strong position to do anything about it, but even so it became his ardent hope that he had not seen the last of Jaubertie. Not that he announced what was on his mind, for Hugh had learned to play his cards close to his chest. But not sufficiently closely, it seemed, to stop others from occasionally catching a glimpse of his hand, as Camilla explains: 'I spoke to my brother's friends during the time when Hugh and my father were not on speaking terms. They all said the same thing, "Your brother is preoccupied by just one thing – he will do *anything* to get Jaubertie."'

It was at this difficult time for the Ryman family that

another wine writer visited the château. It did not take long for Philippe Boucheron, in common with a number of his predecessors, to fall victim to the magic and charm of Jaubertie.

'The Rev'd Sidney Smith got it wrong,' he wrote. 'Paradise is not eating *pâté de foie gras* to the sound of trumpets. It is sitting with Nick Ryman in the garden of Château de la Jaubertie in the tiny village of Colombier, five miles south of Bergerac, tasting his excellent wines and listening to him talk about them with such tremendous enthusiasm.'

Clearly the busy vineyard owner had found time to perfect the role of actor and entertainer. For the truth was that the fifty-seven-year-old *propriétaire* of Jaubertie felt very many miles from paradise, wherever such a place might be. Still struggling with debt and at battle stations with two of the four members of his family, the Englishman had seen his dream sour indeed. It could not even be said that the dream had the nature of a nightmare, because for him there seemed to be no sign at all of that satisfying moment of relief when he would suddenly wake up and realize that the traumatic events troubling him were entirely imaginary.

It was precisely because there seemed to be no light at

the end of his dark and lonely tunnel that Nick Ryman considered the possibility of putting an end to his misery once and for all. Although in his heart he knew that he would have pulled back from the brink, that did not prevent him from frequently wondering whether or not suicide might be the most satisfactory solution of all, and on at least two occasions he toyed with the idea of hurling himself from the bridge at Bergerac into the River Dordogne below. It was at such desperate moments that Jaubertie itself gave the impression of coming to Nick's rescue, its grace and elegance often helping to soothe, comfort and console him.

'These were more than dark moments for me – they were pitch-black. But every-time I would get depressed I would walk up and down the vineyard, very often in the rain, and then come back and look at the château. And I would say to myself, "Come on, Ryman, pull yourself together." You only have to look at the place, smell everything, see everything – especially the wonderful colours of autumn and the views out into the valley of the Dordogne and beyond.'

But Jaubertie alone, despite its undeniable beauty, was not enough. And although an occasional walk in the rain would certainly serve to revive his flagging spirits, the feeling nonetheless persisted for Nick that the purpose of his life had come to an end – that he no longer had any *raison d'être* at all. Always attracted to astrology, he was aware that for Scorpios like himself ambition and a sense of direction were core components which ought never to be far away. Having achieved most of the goals he had set for himself, he seemed to be in precisely the opposite situation, with a distinct lack of enthusiasm for the future.

Had he not built up the family stationery business to the point of making Ryman a household name? And fathered three children, all of whom had grown up into responsible adults, thriving in their respective fields? And having won a whole host of medals and awards for his wines, he had surely proved the point not only that the notion of an Englishman owning and running a vineyard in the Dordogne was not to be scoffed at, but also that the stationer turned wine-maker was perfectly capable of beating the French at their own game. Successes, Nick would muse, but all of them belonged firmly to the past. Most poignant of all though was the fact that he was finding it increasingly difficult to come up with a convincing answer to one question that was constantly on his mind: what on earth was the point of living at Jaubertie alone? Five Rymans had arrived at the château fifteen years earlier, a young family united by happiness and hope. Now only one rather depressed individual remained.

It was with this gloomy and negative outlook on life that Nick accepted an invitation to lunch with some friends. He was introduced to a lady called Sian, who too had every reason to be feeling rather low, for it was almost exactly two years to the day since her husband had passed away. Quite apart from attempting to cope with the ongoing process of mourning, ever since his demise she had been torn between the advice of those who had been urging her to return to England, and those who pleaded with her not to leave the Dordogne.

Sian knew all about Nick Ryman, naturally enough, for he had long since established himself as a well-known local personality, especially among the region's sizeable expatriate English community, and she certainly knew of his wines. There were even mutual friends, although hitherto Nick and Sian's paths had not crossed. When they did, there was an immediate rapport and slowly a close and tender relationship began to develop. She had a natural intelligence and sparkling personality, with which he felt at ease. As Nick explains, 'Meeting

Sian helped to get me through that awful phase of having been alone and in the wilderness. That got me over my first major hurdle and took much of the strain off me as a result. For I had finally found someone who I could really love and who loved me.'

Unlike most people who were happy to see Nick in a relationship again, Camilla did not share the growing consensus of opinion that Sian was the best thing that could have happened to her father. Warm and effusive by nature, Nick's new companion was naturally anxious to win a ringing endorsement of approval from Nick's two daughters. And Corinne was only too pleased to issue hers with no strings attached. Not so Camilla, who found Sian's outgoing nature and chattiness rather difficult to endure, and in her mind muddled a genuine interest in her welfare with a desire to rapidly assume a more maternal role. Since there was clearly no room for such nuances at Château de la Jaubertie, it did not take too long for the underlying tensions to burst out from behind their camouflage of polite conversation, and for an ugly scene to ensue. On the face of it the incident could hardly have been more trivial, triggered off as it was by Sian's desire to see, and Camilla's reluctance to show, the photographs from her recent holiday in the

Maldives. But it could just as easily have been prompted by a thousand other things. Embarrassed by his daughter's lack of courtesy, Nick chose to remain silent – a familiar technique – rather than vent his wrath.

'What's wrong?' Camilla asked the following morning, fully aware of why her father had stopped speaking to her.

'You are so rude,' he replied, breaking his self-imposed silence. 'I cannot forgive you for what you said at dinner last night – I've never seen anyone so rude in my life. I am ashamed you are my daughter.'

'Well, in that case I think that I had better leave now'

'Yes, I think so,' Nick confirmed.

Preparing to set off from the château, Camilla turned to her father, just as Hugh had done a year or so earlier, and decided that the moment had come for him to hear a couple of home truths. 'Well, just before I go, let me tell you one thing,' she said. 'I think that you have never loved us, and you are proving it right now.'

If those harsh words, whether true or not, were designed to overwhelm Nick Ryman with a sudden surge of painful emotion, then they were unsuccessful. For not long after Camilla's sorrowful departure, he confirmed every one of his own remarks in writing, reaffirming the shame and disgust he felt at her behaviour. Not only that, if she ever wanted to see or hear from him again, then she would have to write not one letter of apology but three. One to her father, one to his lady friend, and one to the unfortunate *stagiaire* who had happened to find himself in the line of fire when battle began to rage.

'I wrote back right away and told my father that I was not going to apologize because I was his daughter, that that was the way I am and that therefore he had to accept me as such. I couldn't see why I had to say sorry for having said what I thought. Of course, all of this was happening at the same time as my father was not speaking to Hugh. In fact the only person in the family talking to Daddy was Corinne. It was tough and I felt unhappy. But at the same time it was something I had to do. From that moment on I tried not to think about my father too much. And I would do this by saying one particular phrase. It was the only way I could survive. "My father is dead," I would repeat to myself, "my father is dead."'

Eléonore Isabelle Ryman, however, had a habit of letting all those around her know that she was very much alive. And at no matter what time of the day or night. For on 28 September 1990 Hugh's wife Anne had given birth to a rather plump and full-faced, fair-haired baby girl of nine pounds. But instead of this joyous event serving as a moment of reconciliation between father and son, their three-year war of attrition carried on exactly as it had in the past, with not so much as a single word exchanged between them. Not even the arrival of Nick's first grandchild, it seemed, could be allowed to alter the old entrenched positions.

'You do realize that you are a grandfather?' It was the voice of Esme Johnstone. Having sold his interest in Majestic Wine Warehouses, which he had successfully built up from two to thirty-five stores in eight years, he had decided to settle in France himself, acquiring Château de Sours and its neighbouring vineyards in Entre-Deux-Mers with the proceeds of the sale. The arrival of little Eléonore Ryman in the world happened to be very much on his mind for he had dined with Hugh the night before she was born and lunched with Nick at Jaubertie the day after. Encouraged by his wife Sara, he went on to suggest how fitting it would be not only for peace to break out between the two warring parties, but for Nick to see his granddaughter without further delay. Nick was clearly delighted to have heard of the new arrival – Johnstone even detected a tear or two tucked away in the corner of one eye – and the new grandfather was apparently happy to enquire and talk about the new arrival. But not happy enough, alas, to be able to pick up the phone and dial his son's number in Bordeaux. Neither, for that matter, did Hugh.

Jaubertie too saw a series of new arrivals that year, although not of the human variety. Determined to increase production relative to his fixed costs, and sensing that his wines were at last receiving the

Nick Ryman started producing rosé at Jaubertie in the early 1970s.

recognition they deserved, Nick, encouraged by his partner Charles Martin, embarked on an ambitious programme of buying in crops as a *négociant* from no fewer than ten outside growers. A little too ambitious, as it turned out, because not only did they buy in excessive quantities, but the quality of juice flavours provided by at least two suppliers proved to be entirely unsatisfactory. Nonetheless, although affected by the worldwide recession like many in the trade, Jaubertie continued to break new ground in terms of sales, with a sizeable order from a major supermarket chain, whose buyers were anxious to sell the château's Domaine de Grandchamp, albeit under a special label. Then there were dealings with the off-licence chain Threshers, whose directors had recently acquired the Peter Dominic shops, and who appeared eager to stock Nick's *rosé*, with its intense berry and butterscotch bouquet.

'Jaubertie is a bit like a mistress,' Charles Martin declares, 'a feminine property you can't help but fall in love with. Or at least I couldn't. That was the trouble, in one respect, in that I was no longer able to look at it objectively, in purely commercial terms. I gave my life and soul to that property.'

And not without some success. In the vineyards he

began to closely examine each block of vines: those that tended to have herbaceous characters in their wines he treated in order to increase those characteristics. And those that provided richer fruit he treated similarly, mindful of the importance of having access to better blending material. If only the rest of the process of wine-making was as simple. But even the most sophisticated oenologists are entirely at the mercy of the elements, as both Nick and Charles knew only too well. And in April 1991, as the weather turned against them, disaster struck. Putting pen to paper later that year, shortly after the harvest season had come to a close, Nick broke the bad news to his dedicated band of bondholders, many of whom followed the fluctuating fortunes of Jaubertie as if its vineyards were their own.

'We have just finished our nineteenth *vendange* and it was by far and away the least thrilling,' he wrote. 'Not only did we lose much of our normal crop owing to the frosts earlier in the year, but in the final stages the rain hindered the picking of the Cabernet Sauvignon. We had started picking on 16th September beginning with the Sauvignon. There was the smallest yield imaginable. We continued with the Sémillon and here the yields varied according to the location. In one case we achieved less than 10 hectolitres per hectare against a normal crop of 60. I would estimate that altogether we have lost at least two thirds of our crop.'

One significant effect of that bout of severe weather was the scaling down of their earlier policy of buying in from outside growers. And at Jaubertie itself an equally important decision was taken to reduce crop levels – with a view to making better-quality wines. This had been prompted by an examination of that year's Sauvignon, which, despite its small yield, had produced extremely high-quality grapes, with the most exceptional levels of fruit flavour. This sudden U-turn by the wine-growers might well have been appropriate for competitions and contests, but it was questionable whether or not the same could be said for the key issues of commerce and cash. And for both Nick and Charles alike, it seemed as if the period of their honeymoon was beginning to come to an end.

In Charles Martin's view, there was now a rival for Nick's attention and affection lurking within the vicinity of Jaubertie. 'Perhaps I am being a little bitter when I say this,' Charles admits, 'but things started to go wrong for me when Sian came on the scene, because Nick was devoted to her, and from then on business became pretty much secondary. Nick's forte had always been sales, and he seemed to lose much interest from then on. He did more than take his eye off the ball – out of the stadium, I would say.'

Nick vehemently denies that the rift with Charles was in any way connected with Sian, and points to the cause being an act of professional poor judgement by Charles which led to some economic problems at the château.

If Nick's crops were adversely affected by the frost, then the chances were that the same was true for his son's as well. But unlike the owner of Jaubertie, who was restricted to his property, Hugh was able to look elsewhere. And having conferred with the wine writer Oz Clarke, he decided to look east – to Hungary.

'I have always had a fascination with that part of the world,' he reveals, 'and after the '91 frost it became obvious that cheap wine varieties would be more sought-after. That has always been my approach, to try and think strategically and like that to try and keep ahead of everyone else. I thought that their grapes were likely to taste the same as they do in France – the meat certainly does. So I decided to fly out to Hungary to see if it might be possible to work there.'

What Hugh found at the Gyöngyös estate, eighty kilometres north-east of Budapest, was enough to make his hair stand on end. Mountains of bottles waiting to be filled; fresh juice fermenting immediately after skin contact with no control; at least half a dozen pressings the order of the day; a process of 'blue fining' to remove an imaginary excess of iron; and a stifling system of state control which made the monolithic French social-security system look like a model of streamlined efficiency. But he also discovered a cool climate and low yields, in addition to an impressive attitude among most winemakers. Visiting a number of wineries around the country, Hugh would constantly seek out the response to his much-favoured fruit-flavour test, asking those responsible for production to describe the flavour of the Sauvignon blanc grape, as opposed to the wine. The answers he received were invariably the same: tropical fruit, ivy and ripe apple.

'Each time they said ivy,' he explains, 'I knew that the flavour was at least there in the grape, even if it was not yet obvious in the wine. I tried to convince the director of the state-run cooperative at Gyöngyös to allow us to introduce new-world technology to the old world. It took them a month to agree and to change the style of their wine and to the other changes we were asking for. I say "we" because by then I was working with a number of Australians, a hard-working group of people who are loyal to the end. Together we turned the wine around in a year and sold 70,000 cases in the UK.'

In the world of wine-making this was something akin to a revolution. For before the arrival of Hugh Ryman in Hungary good white wines from countries behind the former Iron Curtain were so rare as to be almost non-existent. Having already been voted as the winner of one White Wine of the Year award, his Gyöngyös Chardonnay was a truly ground-breaking wine for the entire region. Not surprisingly, Hugh's reputation reached new heights. And having learned the art of blowing his own trumpet, or at least allowing others to do it on his behalf, he ensured that these triumphs did not pass by unnoticed. *Wine* magazine was quick to hail Hugh as 'one of France's most promising young wine-makers', while to the *Mail on Sunday* he was nothing less than a 'wine wizard' whose globe-trotting feet hardly ever touched the ground as he went about his business of turning tired wines into some of the best vintages around.

With a spate of such publicity it was difficult for Nick

not to chart the course of Hugh's career, even though father and son were by then poised to enter the fourth year of their feud. As he read one article after another highlighting Hugh's achievements, part of Nick was proud of his son. And part of him was not.

'Hugh was becoming more and more of a star. He was not the flavour of the month, but the flavour of the decade. The spotlight was always on Hugh – young, good-looking, calmer in his approach and less black and white than me. I began to feel as if people were trying to ignore the fact that I had ever existed. And at the same time I was quietly happy to see what a success he was making. I didn't say anything, but quietly I was proud.'

Nick would also have had every reason to be proud of Camilla. But, as with her brother, the stalemate of silence prevailed. Having graduated from the University of Paris, she had managed to find a job in the field of public relations, where her skills as a linguist and an effective communicator were soon put to good use. She had also become deeply involved in a relationship with a young man called Henry Chevalier, who, with his father, ran a male model agency in the French capital. Camilla really needed to speak to her father about her future with Henry and rather urgently at that, on the grounds that it was their intention to be wed. She informed him of her decision by post.

Two months later Camilla's letter remained unanswered. Determined to resolve the matter once and for all, she picked up the phone and tapped out the ten digits for Jaubertie. Her nervousness was only partially reduced when she realized that it was Charles Martin on the other end of the line.

'Could I speak to my father, please?' she said. After a few moments she heard his voice.

'What do you want?' Nick asked, his tone abrupt and abrasive. 'Did you get my letter?'

'Yes, and I don't care.'

And with those words Nick hung up. Camilla immediately called again, merely to have the phone put down on her a second time. Only on her next attempt was it possible to continue the conversation, although from her point of view it was far from a case of third time lucky.

'Daddy was pretty unpleasant. He said some rather nasty things about Henry, and told me that he didn't want a family wedding at Jaubertie. The only time I got in touch, he said, was to ask for money or count the silver spoons, which simply wasn't true. Daddy seemed to be going through a paranoid phase – convincing himself that we all wanted him to die so as to be able to get our hands on his money. And it became more obvious to me than ever that Charles Martin had become his replacement son. "But Daddy," I said, "blood is thicker than water." To which he replied: "What are you talking about – and who wants a family anyway?" When I put the phone down for the fourth and final time I was devastated. In fact I didn't sleep for an entire week.'

There were seldom such displays of emotion, however, from brother Hugh. He had developed the knack of keeping his feelings firmly under control – an ability no doubt acquired during his first few terms as a boarder at public school. Nonetheless, when he heard from two separate sources that the château was on the market, even he found it difficult to maintain his cool composure. Ever since he had fallen out with his father five years earlier, his long-term strategy had been to ensure that the home in which he had lived for at least a decade should remain firmly within the Ryman family. Suddenly everything he had been working towards appeared to be in turmoil and under threat. Suddenly, far from his having the time to indulge in procrastination and posturing – the hallmark of the recent past – it became imperative for him to make contact with his father right away. Picking up the phone, he wondered if he was likely to be received any more favourably than his sister. It hardly seemed likely. But then, he reminded himself, his objectives were entirely different. For it was not peace and friendship with which he was expecting to emerge – but the title deeds of Jaubertie.

HEALTH
AND
WEALTH

11

JOSEPH BACCO'S HIPS were troubling him; they had been for some time. At first, the fifty-three-year-old Italian *chef de culture* tried to ignore the swelling and stiffness in those two crucial joints, convincing himself that the accompanying bouts of pain would pass. But they did not. In fact, unbeknown to him, the firm cartilage they once contained had long since begun to flake and crack, thickening and distorting the underlying bone. Determined as he was to tough it out, it was to take Joseph some time to admit, both to himself and those around him, that his condition was deteriorating rather than improving with the passage of time.

Only when it had come to the point of finding himself hobbling around the vineyard, instead of proceeding at his usual brisk and breezy pace, was Joseph prepared to heed the oft-repeated advice of his wife Agnès, that it was high time he sought out specialist advice. By the time he did so, osteoarthritis was so advanced that it was impossible to consider any treatment other than hip replacement. While the doctors were unable to point to a precise cause for the condition, no one was in any doubt that thirty-five years of hard graft in the vineyards had taken their toll. Then Joseph was given a medical opinion which frightened him considerably more than the prospect of being at the receiving end of a surgeon's knife. Despite a ninety per cent success rate in such operations, he was told, there could be no question of his returning to tend the vines of Jaubertie. Those days were over.

'It broke my heart to stop working,' Joseph admits. 'But I had no choice. I asked Monsieur Ryman to make me redundant actually, because this was more attractive financially than simply going off sick. Like that I would be entitled to receive a lump sum as well as being able to claim invalidity allowance. He didn't have to go along with this suggestion, but he did. In fact he was more than generous with me – without doubt the best employer I have ever had in the whole of my working life.'

No doubt it is the natural order of things. For just as Joseph's career was coming to a close, so his son François' was in the ascendant. To some extent this was attributable to Hugh, who, before his departure from Jaubertie, had promoted his erstwhile playmate and accomplice in mischief of all kinds from the humble status of *ouvrier* to the more prestigious rank of *maître de chais*, or cellar master. Not much changed in terms of François' daily workload, but it was due recognition of seven solid years of service and the accompanying rise in salary was particularly welcome, for François already had a number of commitments of his own. Two years younger than his English friend, he had also married two years before him, having taken his marriage vows just a couple of weeks before his twenty-first birthday, which coincided with Christmas Day. Nor had he been obliged to stray far from the château to meet his future wife. He had first noticed the unfamiliar but attractive face and figure of Fabienne Harribelçague, whose dark eyes and curly brown hair hinted at her Basque ancestry, at the annual *fête de la cantine*, the local primary school's main event, which traditionally took place on 8 May in the playground of the school at

Labadie. Fabienne, from Bordeaux, happened to be spending the weekend with her grandmother, whose local credentials were beyond dispute, being a resident of Bouniagues, only a few kilometres away.

'When I met François for the first time,' says Henry Mondié, 'he was a young boy who had just turned eleven years old. And it never crossed my mind then that ten years later I would be marrying him in my capacity as mayor.'

It had not taken Henry long to become a polished performer while officiating at such occasions, and with François and Fabienne and their families crammed into the tiny *mairie* of Colombier, he had had no difficulty in striking a satisfactory balance between solemn ceremonial and subtle celebration. 'But I can assure everyone here today,' he had gone on to say, 'that if François works as hard at his marriage as he does at Château de la Jaubertie, then all I can see is a very rosy future indeed.'

Those words had proved to be particularly well chosen, for not only did the newly-weds settle down in a happy and successful partnership, but two years later they were blessed with Marjorie, a little girl, born in Bergerac like her father. And then, two years after that, Romain arrived, a son at last. The Baccos had also managed to borrow sufficient funds from the Crédit

Agricole with which to have their own house built. Only a short drive from Jaubertie, it could easily be seen standing proudly in the valley below the *métairie*, the single-storey farmhouse situated within the grounds of the château in which François had spent many of his formative years.

'If Hugh has done well,' he explains, 'it is because he has worked hard and is clever. He has a gift for wine-making, there's no doubt about that. Next to him I feel very small. But I also know that he had a lot of problems while growing up. That's why when Hugh left Jaubertie in 1987 I was convinced that he would never come back. Not after all their rows together.'

Which only served to illustrate the extent to which the two young men, although both now husbands and fathers in their own right, had come to drift apart. For, unbeknown to François, after five years of silence in public and as many years of recrimination in private, his former fishing and shooting partner had finally plucked up the courage to renew contact with his father by telephoning him at Jaubertie.

'It was difficult to pick up the receiver,' Hugh admits. 'But if you want to make something work – then where there is a will there is a way. My main interest was to keep Jaubertie in the family. That was my priority, rather than attempting to salvage things with my father. In so far as that was concerned the damage had been done – disinheriting and all that. You don't forgive that sort of thing too easily. By this time I had my own family, our second daughter Maud having been born in the January of 1992, so maybe I didn't need the external family any more. I suppose I must have grown up. I just began to find the whole thing extremely childish.'

'Father,' Hugh began, 'I think we should talk. I would also be interested to know why Jaubertie is going on the market. Is it due to financial matters or what?'

Perhaps Nick was shrewd enough to see through his son's strategy, and took the view that a peace overture motivated partly by commercial considerations was simply not a satisfactory basis for the laying down of arms. Or perhaps he was too proud and unyielding to entertain the prospect of being seen to back-pedal in any way, for their frosty relations had long since passed into the public domain. Whatever the case, Nick soon gave his son short shift. 'I don't think there is anything to talk about,' he replied.

Another six months were required before Nick was prepared to modify his harsh and inflexible stance. For during that period the feeling intensified that his days of making wine at Jaubertie were coming to a close. Just as he had sought a new challenge after twenty years of building up the Ryman stationery stores, so after twenty vintages the old enthusiasm which had propelled him on during his earlier days at the château was no longer there. When Hugh telephoned again, therefore, in the summer of 1992, he found that Nick had changed his tune.

'Father, I really do think that we should have a talk.'

'Yes, why not,' Nick replied, always a man of few words.

Meeting in the restaurant of the stylish three-star Hôtel du Château at Lalinde, situated up-river from Jaubertie and overlooking the banks of the Dordogne, father and son did precisely that, interrupting their conversation only to eat, drink wine and uncork a half bottle of champagne to finish off the meal. Five hours later, they were still at it, as if attempting to make up for the five lost years.

'I thought that we wouldn't be noticed,' Nick recalls. 'But within half an hour the whole of the Dordogne knew what was happening, including what we had eaten and practically every word we had spoken.'

But Hugh failed to come away from that lengthy

lunch with what was uppermost in his mind. In fact Nick hardly gave his son's offer – one million francs per annum over a period of ten years – the time of day, on the grounds that he was more interested in receiving a larger lump sum right away. Besides, there were a number of other options in the pipeline. All that Hugh could extract from his father was the promise that he would be the first to be informed should there be any developments relating to the sale of Jaubertie.

'I would never have forgiven my father for having sold the château without having been given the chance to make a bid. It is an exquisite property with a lot of charisma and I felt that I might be able to get it back on the right track. My position was quite straightforward: if he would have disposed of it without honouring that pledge, then I would never have spoken to him again.'

Not that that would have changed matters much from the pattern of the previous years. Nonetheless, although Hugh appeared to have emerged with precisely the opposite of what he had set out to achieve – partial peace but with only a remote prospect of being able to acquire the château – at least the festering boil of bitterness, the consequences of which affected three generations of Rymans rather than two, had been successfully lanced and seemed unlikely to turn septic again.

For Joseph Bacco, adjusting to the concept of enforced early retirement on health grounds was a slow and painful process. Just as he was beginning to do so, his former *patron* was noticing that he too was far from in fighting shape, finding it difficult on occasions to draw breath. But unlike Joseph, who had spent a considerable time denying that he was in need of medical attention, Nick immediately headed off to his local doctor, who in turn sent him to a health centre in Bergerac, where he was advised to undergo a stress test right away. In view of the traumas Nick had experienced during the previous few years, his rating really ought to have been right off the upper end of the scale. But it was not. On the contrary, it revealed this his heart was functioning perfectly well, although the wisdom of cutting back on his intake of nicotine and alcohol was pointed out.

As the months went by, however, these apparently satisfactory results appeared to be at odds with reality. Because for Nick Ryman even the most elementary of tasks, such as walking up a flight of stairs, had become major undertakings, requiring him to sit down and thoroughly assess the challenge before proceeding. It was the same story when mowing the lawn at Jaubertie: only the smallest section could be completed before he was obliged to rest and recover his breath. And on one occasion he had found himself staggering towards the nearest chair, clutching his chest in pain. On returning to his doctor for a second and more urgent consultation, he was told to book an appointment with Professor Clémenty, one of France's leading heart specialists, who was based in Pessac, a sprawling suburb of Bordeaux. Nick was hardly impressed to find out that he would have to wait a further three months before being able to see him, but there was little he could do about it.

It was at this time that Hugh Ryman and Esme Johnstone decided to combine their various commercial interests, as well as their names, through the creation of the Rystone Group. It was their belief that Hugh's technical skills as a wine-maker, together with Esme's financial expertise, would make them a much more potent force in the highly competitive wine market. Merging their companies also put them in a more effective position to be able to raise working capital – capital with which they hoped to be able to acquire Château de la Jaubertie. And now that father and son

In his twenty-year career Nick Ryman succeeded in improving dramatically the standard of Bergerac's previously indifferent wines, and in doing so won several awards.

were on speaking terms again Esme wasted no time in entering into negotiations with Nick about the possibility of the newly formed group – part of which was owned by a subsidiary of Hambros Bank – buying the château outright. Quite apart from his underlying malaise, Nick's ill health naturally helped in the process of concentrating his mind, and never more so than the moment when he was informed that a four-part heart-bypass operation would have to be performed as a matter of urgency.

'At the hospital they told me to come back the following day,' Nick relates, 'and that they were going to take me to pieces more or less right away. I said, "You can't do that, I have business to attend to." They said, "Well, it must be pretty important business." I was still negotiating with Esme and Hugh. In the end I agreed to be admitted a fortnight later. During this time I got hold of them both and said, "Look, we had better get something pretty clear soon, before I go into hospital, because I might not come out." We then signed a *promesse de vente* which was agreed at a semi-official meeting with a *notaire*, and in which it was simply stated that they wished to buy and that I wished to sell – but nothing more elaborate than that. Of course all of this didn't put me in a very strong negotiating position in so far as the sale of the château was concerned. But I was tired and to some extent my feeling was that I had lived my life.'

As Nick was contemplating what the future might hold, Camilla was doing likewise a few hundred miles away in Paris. She was at a friend's house, where, as had happened on previous occasions, a set of tarot cards was being used as an instrument of fortune-telling. In the past Camilla had not taken these proceedings too seriously until the end of her romance with Henry Chevalier had been predicted with an uncanny degree of accuracy. And although that relationship had since been revived, she had gone on to suspend all judgement as to whether or not the cards, with their pictures portraying vices and virtues of various kinds, were to be believed or not. That autumn evening it was the turn of another girl, a stranger to Camilla, to select the cards. As she did so, she began to speak about an important house that was going to change hands; of difficulties in relation to a transaction; and of a person who travelled a lot. The tarot reader then turned towards Camilla and said, 'I know that all this is really important for you, but you will have some news very quickly.' Intrigued by these apparent references to Hugh's battle to buy Jaubertie, Camilla had failed to notice the hours slipping by. And she rang her boyfriend at their flat in the third *arrondissement* to inform him that she was likely to be delayed for dinner.

'You'll never guess who phoned,' Henry said, barely able to contain his news.

'No.'

'Your father.'

'I think I must have gone into shock,' Camilla relates. 'I had to sit down. It had been three years since we had fallen out. I phoned back the next day and Daddy just said, "Let's forget the whole thing." Of course I agreed. He then told me that he had been in pain and that he was shortly to undergo major heart surgery. So while I was pleased to have heard from him, at the same time I was sorry that it had to be with bad news. I told him how happy I was that he had got in touch. And he replied, "I just thought you might want to know."'

'SEE THE MAN WHO HAS FAITH'

12

IT WAS IN November 1993 that Nick Ryman was wheeled off towards an operating theatre in the high-tech cardiac unit of the Hôpital du Haut-Lévèque. An ample supply of relaxants had already been administered to the *propriétaire* of Jaubertie, who was more than ready to enter into the battle for his life. Aware that an incision would shortly be made down the centre of his chest, his ribcage sawn through and opened up, he was confident that, while his heart was stopped for the bypass to be performed, his circulation and breathing would be taken over by a state-of-the-art heart and lung machine.

In the event the operation went smoothly enough,

although the aftermath of the surgery itself was less satisfactory, as Camilla explains: 'After the operation I telephoned Daddy. Sian was there, and she was fantastic. But when I heard that he had contracted an infection I became very worried. Eventually I went to visit him with Corinne at his *maison de repos* in the Pays Basque. I was scared to see him again. But instead of being in bed as I had expected he was dressed and sitting up. He looked fine – just as I'd left him three years before. There were a few bottles of wine in the room – the wine had helped to fur his arteries up in the first place.' Corinne Ryman adds: 'It was the sugar in the alcohol – together with many years of worry and stress. In fact when we were visiting I was sent out to buy the *apéritifs* from a nearby supermarket, on the grounds that he wouldn't drink what was provided by the home. He was under strict orders – a maximum of one quarter of a bottle of wine per meal – completely ignored by Daddy, needless to say.'

A few months later Nick was feeling as right as rain. Ever the car enthusiast, he was soon showing off to friends and family alike. 'It's the same old bodywork,' he would joke, 'but with a new engine inside.' The process of healing then received an additional boost when, shortly before the spring of 1994, Camilla and Henry announced, although not for the first time, that they were to be wed. Despite the recent outbreak of peace and goodwill, however, it was not long before it became evident that attempting to forget the past was easier said than done. For the notion that it would not be possible for her to marry at the château where she had grown up had evidently become firmly fixed in the prospective bride's mind. Jaubertie had once been deemed out of bounds to Camilla by her father; Jaubertie was where her brother had married; Jaubertie was the setting where her parents' marriage had subsequently failed and her mother would not be welcome there. It was clear that an alternative, less problematic place would have to be found.

Just as Camilla was striking the château which she loved off her list as an appropriate venue, so her niece, now three and a half years old, could hardly wait to set foot there for the first time. Little Eléonore Ryman had seen the handsome house often enough – but only as a backdrop to her parents' wedding photographs. And she had occasionally asked about the identity of one particular face which was unfamiliar to her – grandfather Nick's. Not that her parents had ever sought to be secretive in any way. But with Camilla's wedding only three months away, they took the view that the time had come for their two daughters to meet both Sian and Nick. Far better to get to know one another now, they thought, than meeting on the wedding day for the first time. So the four Rymans duly set off from Bordeaux, driving east towards Bergerac and the Dordogne. Five Rymans, in fact, for Hugh's wife Anne was by then seven months pregnant with her third child. It was to be a moment of some significance for the young doctor too, returning as she was to Jaubertie after an absence of seven years. In the event everything took place with undue fuss or awkwardness, although it was plain for all to see that Nick was deeply moved to set eyes on his two delightful granddaughters. For both Eléonore and Maud alike there was not the slightest difficulty in accepting and embracing their father's father, whom they spontaneously dubbed Nicholas, rather than Grandpère or Papi.

'So where is the wedding to take place?' Sian would often ask. With the marriage approaching fast, it was not an unreasonable question. Camilla was perfectly capable of providing the answer, yet she seemed to be reluctant to do so. It was as if there was some sort of psychological block between the processes of thought and speech, for the information simply failed to flow – most out of character for Camilla.

'Oh, at a house in the country,' she would offer.

'Yes, but who does the house belong to?'

'Well, it's a friend of mummy's,' Camilla would venture deliberately telling the truth but not the whole truth.

'And what's this person's name?'

'Jean-Louis Lesage.'

And Nick was just as likely to join in these ad hoc interrogations. 'What was that man's name again?' he would sometimes ask. 'What did you say he does for a living?' He would follow up with a number of other questions along the same lines.

'It was all terribly *délicat*,' Camilla recalls. 'I didn't want to hurt my father by broadcasting the fact that I was getting married at mummy's boyfriend's country house in the Gironde. And that that was where I had been spending my weekends during the years when I wasn't speaking to him. But at the same time I was aware that he was going to have to find out sooner or later.'

As for the flying wine-maker, he had no difficulty at all in living up to his name. He might begin his working day with a visit to Germany in the morning – stop, taste, organize and plan – then in the evening fly off to the Hincesti winery in Moldova, seventy kilometres from the Romanian border, where his company was responsible for the making of a muscular Chardonnay in a joint venture with Penfolds. Only to be back in Bordeaux again the next day. Or there would be the occasional three-day trip to South Africa, South America or San Francisco as part of a wide range of consultancy contracts secured by the Rystone Group.

Together with his partner Esme Johnstone, whose own Château de Sours had been incorporated into the group, Hugh had succeeded in increasing his turnover of wine from 150,000 cases in 1988 to in excess of one and a half million six years later. It was a remarkable achievement: the vinification of 2000 hectares in various parts of the world – the equivalent of approximately forty Jauberties.

'I have never considered myself to be a gifted wine-maker in any way,' Hugh declares. 'My role is simply to audit the nineteen wine-makers we have. We lay down the policy, say where we want to go, true. But now, as soon as one of our wine-makers has made a good wine people think that I have made it, which is not necessarily the case at all. Only when you have made something like a Mas de Daumas Gassac or a Château Margaux will you be able to turn round and say that you have created a classic, something that will stand the test of time, like a great painting. I haven't done that. None of our wines are great in that sense. But what I do say is that they are certainly the best we could have made from the fruit we had and for the price we ask.'

So busy, then, but still with plenty of time to fix his eyes firmly on Jaubertie. Because of the turbulent past between father and son, and in view of Esme's experience in the world of finance, it was decided that the tall, bluff Old Harrovian would continue to lead the negotiations for the acquisition of Jaubertie on behalf of the Rystone Group. Not that anything was agreed upon speedily. On the contrary, after several months of talks and meetings of various kinds, there were still no signs of any signatures at all, with the all-important *acte définitif* apparently as elusive as ever.

In some respects many of the discussions taking place about the forthcoming wedding were more complex than the protracted negotiations for Jaubertie, in that their subject matter was families and feelings rather than fortunes and finance. Aware of her father's capacity for sudden flashes of anger and unpredictable behaviour, Camilla could only hope that Saturday 11 June 1994 would not prove to be one of his off-days. However, when she arrived at Jaubertie on the Thursday before the celebrations were due to begin, a number of her worst fears were confirmed. For when the sensitive subject of seating in church came up, Nick found himself unwilling to restrain himself, especially on the subject of his mother-in-law. 'So where do you think grandma should sit then?' Camilla enquired, aware that her father had not seen or spoken to Isobel Butters since her final abrupt departure from Jaubertie some years earlier.

'I'll tell you where we'll place your grandmother,' Nick replied, as irascible as ever. 'We'll put her in front of everyone all on her own.' If that was a foretaste of things to come, Camilla thought, then how on earth was her father going to react when introduced to JeanLouis Lesage, his estranged wife's lover, quite apart from the prospect of being received as a guest in his home? It hardly seemed to augur well for the big day.

As Nick dusted down his top hat and tails, however, he knew that he had every reason to feel proud. He had produced wines of such elegance that Bergerac could no longer be shrugged off merely as a minor extension to its mighty neighbour St Émilion. And he had every intention of ensuring that at least one Jaubertie wine would be served on his daughter's wedding day. Perhaps even the late Alexis Lichine, the so called 'Pope of wine', having once passed Bergerac off as 'a countryside that has more appeal to the eye than the wines do to the palate', might have had reason to reassess his rather haughty judgement. Twenty-two years earlier, when Nick Ryman had first set out to fulfil his dream, many a local *viticulteur* had confidently predicted that the Englishman would be bankrupt in next to no time at all. While those forecasts of failure had come perilously close, he had somehow managed to stave off such a fate, sometimes through inspired judgements on his part, but more often through sheer stubbornness and grit. How the tables had turned, for now they came to him for advice. A local wine agent, Patrick Montfort, explains.

There are currently ten to fifteen vineyards in the area following the path already trodden by Monsieur Ryman. He was the first to believe in the quality of Bergerac wines. And being an outsider made it all the more difficult for him, because he wasn't always very well thought of by the local wine establishment, Le Conseil interprofessionnel des vins de la région de Bergerac. He has proved himself to be a pioneer in the field, raising the level of Bergerac wines as a whole.'

As if to publicly proclaim their new-found peace, it was agreed between father and son that Nick would supply the red wine for the wedding, his acclaimed Réserve Rouge, with its attractive berry fruit and integrated oak flavour, while Hugh would do likewise for the whites, selecting a Chardonnay from the Cave du Casse at Limoux, in addition to his Petits Grains Muscat as a sweet dessert wine.

When Nick arrived in the small village of Aillas, situated halfway between Bordeaux and Agen, he made an entrance to remember. Determined not to drive on his daughter's wedding day, he had taken it upon himself to hire transport so that the contingent of guests setting out from the Dordogne would be able to do exactly as he intended – drink as much as they pleased without having to worry about driving. After some consideration he had decided to go ahead and rent the only vehicle he managed to find available on that day, on the grounds that a large coach was better than no coach at all. Nonetheless the sight of Nick and Sian, together with just four other smartly clad couples, alighting from a huge blue and white, twelve-ton fifty-seater succeeded in raising more than the odd eyebrow in Aillas. Still, at least everyone in the village knew that the father of the bride was present and accounted for.

Which was more than could be said for the groom, Henry Chevalier. For when Camilla arrived at the *mairie* in order to take part in the civil ceremony, he was nowhere to be seen, which came as something of a surprise to the twenty-six-year-old public relations officer. Not that the absence of the groom seemed to distress Nick, who, to Camilla's relief, appeared to have arrived in the very best of spirits. Deciding to make the most of the glorious sunshine that day, he suggested that the advance party install themselves in the local café, where he immediately ordered several bottles of champagne, toasting his daughter's health before the official celebrations had begun.

'I didn't want a grandiose wedding like Hugh,' Camilla explains. 'All I was hoping for was a simple country wedding, stripped of starchiness and officialdom of all kind.'

The ninth-century chapel situated in Aillas-le-Vieux certainly met these criteria, since it had been built and remained in the middle of an open field, from where a herd of cows would occasionally interrupt their grazing to cast a doleful eye on the excited activity all around. The church itself was not without interest, principally because of the presence of an old wooden boat, precariously suspended from the ceiling for the best part of two centuries, and all the more remarkable given that the village is many miles from the sea. The local people were always happy to explain this rather baffling sight and to tell the story of how the vessel had come to be there: in the mid-eighteenth century it was said, a sailor had found himself in the midst of a terrible storm in the Atlantic, one so powerful that he became convinced he would not survive. And he prayed to St Marie of Aillas – who had evidently answered his prayers – for the grateful sailor had subsequently made a gift of the boat as a token of his appreciation. The chapel had become a place of pilgrimage ever since.

Then another miracle, albeit lower down the spiritual scale: Henry Chevalier had made an appearance after all. He was simply late. Then all eyes turned towards Camilla as she prepared to walk down the aisle of the chapel constructed over a thousand years earlier during the reign of Charlemagne. Dressed in a full-length white skirt and matching jacket, but without a single piece of jewellery, she looked exceptionally radiant, her fair hair swept back and tucked up in a bun, accentuating her fine bone structure and giving the impression of an attractive and confident young woman blessed with the qualities of grace, elegance and ease.

'Going into the church was the most difficult moment of all,' she says, 'knowing that everyone was waiting and looking at me. But I was happy to be with Daddy, knowing that after all that had happened between us he was taking me to give me away to Henry.'

With both the civil and religious proceedings out of the way, the congregation headed towards the country home of Jean-Louis Lesage, where a lavish meal for the 200 guests was being prepared, with the party scheduled to begin at 6.30 that evening. Just as she had decided to give herself a day off from catering at Hugh's wedding, so the bride's mother Anne was happy to hand over responsibility for all matters culinary to a caterer from the Landes, whose delicious bacon and prune confections and *brochette*-style langoustine and prawns served during cocktails promised an excellent meal to follow. In fact Anne Ryman was very moved to see her husband again, for despite their years apart neither person had sought to initiate divorce proceedings. It was the first time Anne and Nick had seen each other since

Anne's abrupt departure from Jaubertie six years earlier.

'I was just hoping that Daddy wasn't going to have one of his fits,' Camilla admits. 'I know that he has this incredible capacity to sometimes go over the top, and all I could do was to keep my fingers crossed that he would be agreeable, especially with my mother and grandmother. But on D-day he was just amazing – perfect, actually. Charming, friendly and open – I couldn't believe it. For me it was like a fairy tale coming true, and I remember thinking to myself, how wonderful, everything is over.'

It was a perspective not necessarily shared by the bride's mother. For while Anne was happy enough in her new relationship with Jean-Louis, just as Nick was with Sian, it was clear that she was still mourning the loss of Jaubertie. And seeing Nick again, whom she continued to respect and admire in spite of the breakdown of their marriage, threw these issues into sharp relief, triggering off unfinished business from the past.

'It's difficult to explain the extraordinary effect that Jaubertie has had on us all,' she reflects. 'In some ways its hold is rather frightening. I still consider Jaubertie to be my home, and I suppose I always will. I don't think I shall ever get over the fact that I no longer live there.'

At Jean-Louis' country house – named Montmartre in common with the part of Paris famed for its artists and cafés – a veritable banquet was being served to the accompaniment of Nick and Hugh's wines. Although the main course was *canard farci*, there seemed to be an unlimited supply of *foie gras*, salmon and salads, with a *fraisier* waiting to be served as dessert for those who could still find the room.

When Nick rose to his feet to make a speech, he immediately demonstrated a generosity of spirit that charmed everyone present, thanking Jean-Louis for his readiness to make his home available for the wedding reception. In fact it appeared as if Nick was locked into goodwill mode, as he proceeded to move around the specially constructed dance floor first with his daughter, then his wife, eventually surpassing himself by asking his mother-in-law to accompany him too. Whatever next?

Esme Johnstone was among the guests that evening. Even though he was in the throes of negotiating the purchase of Jaubertie on behalf of the Rystone Group, he too could not help but admire the man with whom he had spent many a long hour haggling over the sale.

'He created something for himself, from a standing start,' he affirms, 'to the point that Jaubertie now has a worldwide reputation. Even the French in Bergerac would freely admit that Jaubertie is the best wine made there by a million miles, and that it has been a fantastic advert for the *appellation* as a whole. To me the world is made up of two types of people: salary earners, who take the 8.45 train to Waterloo every morning. And then there is another category of person who is prepared to step into the unknown, and take an almighty risk. Nick comes into that second group and on principle I admire people like that. Of course to do that you have to be prepared to take responsibility for your actions because if things go wrong, then the buck stops with you. Anyone who makes that step over the divide has got to be a maverick, at least to some degree. A business going from the soil, all the way to a customer sitting in a restaurant drinking your wine in Japan. Not many businesses are as all-embracing as that. So if I were Nick Ryman I would feel as if I could hold my head high come the day of reckoning.'

The youngest guest present that evening was undoubtedly Edwin Ryman, four weeks old to the day. Although his mother had not sought to ask about the sex of the unborn baby, her medical training had enabled her to discreetly study the shadow images of the scans taken during her pregnancy and conclude that the chances were she was carrying a son – a secret she shared with no one, not even her husband Hugh. In common with his partner Esme, Camilla's wedding day was for Hugh a time for reflection as well as celebration.

'Looking back on my father's dream I would say that you live by your mistakes. To me a father should be there as someone you can talk to, someone with whom you can share a personal or professional problem. That was something which I never had. So even during our "wilderness years" I didn't really lose that much, because there wasn't that much to lose in the first place. But fortunately the family has now come together again, at least in a manner of speaking. I think that my father's operation helped in this respect, because he definitely thought that his time was up.'

As the evening progressed and it became clear that each event had been a huge success, Camilla finally felt free to let her hair down, joining in the dancing with the broadest possible smile. Having spent her wedding night in a modern hotel in Bouliac, just outside Bordeaux, she returned the following day to Montmartre for lunch where, naturally enough, she found a very different scene. Apart from her mother and grandmother, everyone had gone. Nick had returned to the Dordogne in his coach with Sian and a handful of other guests. Hugh had left for Bordeaux with his wife, two daughters and new-born son. Corinne was already back in Paris with her Greek boyfriend Dimitri. Relieved that her family had managed to put their differences behind them, she could now allow herself to look forward to enjoying a rather extravagant two-part honeymoon, a few days in New York followed by a holiday in Morocco. While she drew comfort from the fact that it was the first time the five Rymans had come together for many years, she also knew that the likelihood of their doing so again was extremely remote, at least for the foreseeable future. Hardly surprising then, that Camilla should have experienced a surge of sorrow as she realized that her fifteen-hour fairy tale had come to an end.

Tending to the gardens of his substantial property in High Wycombe, Desmond Ryman was disappointed not to have been able to be present at his niece's wedding. But with Cicely suffering with severe back pain at the time, there had been no question of the couple undertaking the journey to France. Nevertheless, his thoughts had been with the rest of the Rymans that day, and especially with his brother Nick.

'I've only recently come to understand why Nick stopped communicating with me ever since the day we sold the business to Burtons,' he admits. 'Previously we used to be so close – we did everything together. Although it is my firm belief that he considerably understates his own role in the building up of our stationery chain, if that was his perception, then I can see that it was entirely understandable that he should want to go off and do something different, without involving his big brother in any way. And therefore to prove to himself that he was perfectly capable of doing his own thing – which he has done. I take my hat off to him. But I still believe that Jaubertie was far too big in the first place and that because he always insisted on it being perfect in every way he poured much more money into it than ought to have been the case. So if he did eventually make a success of it, it has been at the expense of his marriage, his health and every penny he has ever had.'

With Nick continuing to normalize relations with his son, it was almost inevitable that Charles Martin would in due course have to step aside. And within a few weeks of Camilla's wedding he had left Jaubertie to set up shop on his own. Not that he abandoned the Dordogne, for he immediately established a company called Château de la Colline, situated at Thénac, near Sigoulès, where he set about applying his considerable talents to the making of his own reds, whites and *rosés*. Unlike Jaubertie, however, there was no sign of any château to be seen at Charles's new venture.

'I disposed of my shares in Jaubertie as part of an understanding to get out. Nick was very generous with me. He always has been. I left to do my own thing – the time was right, especially since there was a lot of uncertainty at that time. I was aware that Hugh and Esme were negotiating to buy the château, apart from which my relationship with Nick had long since gone sour – ever since Sian came along, really. Nick and I had a spectacular row together and I was no longer really happy in my work.'

Nick's recollections, on the other hand, are that the cause of the problem was not Sian but Charles's unfeeling arrogance. He turned to Charles and said that he was selling Jaubettie and that Charles must look for another job.

On Friday, 7 October 1994, twenty-one years, one week and a day after he had acquired Château de la Jaubertie, Nick Ryman travelled into Bergerac in order to formally dispose of it. The same firm of notaries responsible for the handling of the original transaction was appointed to deal with the conveyance. It had taken over a year to finalize the precise terms, but in the event it was agreed that Hugh and Esme's Rystone Group would pay for the château and its vineyards over seven years, with Nick having the right to remain and live at Jaubertie for a minimum of three. Punctual as always, he arrived on his own, just as he had done over two decades earlier when completing the purchase from the Sauvats. Then Esme walked into the office with his wife Sara, where a tax specialist, an accountant and a translator were already in attendance. And finally Hugh arrived, approximately half an hour late, as is his wont, together with his wife Anne. As impatient as Nick had originally been to become the owner of the château, so now he could hardly wait for the transfer of the title to go through.

'This meeting was meant to begin at 10 o'clock,' he announced. 'We must finish before 12.30. Because that is when I intend to leave.'

With that rather brusque remark having the desired

effect of concentrating the minds of all concerned, the meeting finally got underway. It was the responsibility of the *notaire* to ensure that the implications and consequences of every term and condition contained in the contract were comprehensible to purchasers and vendor alike. 'Monsieur Ryman, you do understand what is meant by this clause?' he would occasionally enquire of Nick.

While Nick was naturally aware of the main points of the deal he had struck, he had not concerned himself unduly with reading the small print of the legal document before him.

'Yes, I do,' he would reply rather convincingly. 'Can we move on, please?'

'We rose at 12.30,' Nick relates. 'Once we had all signed the *acte définitif*, I thought, thank God for that. They say that a week is a long time in politics: well, twenty years in a vineyard is too long as well. Immediately I felt free again. No responsibilities other than the upkeep of the lawn. I was then taken out for a very nice lunch in Castillonnès. From that moment on I knew that my greatest dilemma was going to be "to mow or not to mow" – nothing more worrying than that.'

'Of course it was satisfying coming back and buying

my father out,' Hugh admits. 'It was as if things had come full circle. It felt good to know that in some areas at least I was right. But I didn't want it to be seen as rescuing Jaubertie, or indeed as having humiliated my father in any way – merely the continuation of an established business.'

'To me it seems a little strange that a son has to buy out his father,' Corinne reflects. 'Normally in France an asset such as the château would in due course be passed on to all three children. But at the same time I was glad that Hugh bought Jaubertie – at least like that it stays within the family. Looking back at my father's dream I think that overall it was a good thing. People should remember though that it was the two of them, Mummy and Daddy together, perhaps even the five of us. It took courage and I have loved it, despite everything we have all been through.'

For over twenty years the great dreamer himself had no idea of the significance of the escutcheon bearing the Latin words *'Vide Cui Fides'* which, for centuries, had been associated with Château de la Jaubertie. And even though he had gone to the trouble of having those three words reproduced on every item of the château's elegant, red-rimmed Royal Worcester dinner service, he had always remained ignorant as to their precise meaning. It was not for want of trying, but a number of enquiries had indicated that it was not a particularly easy phrase to translate. Only once he had disposed of his interest in Jaubertie did he discover that those hitherto incomprehensible words could hardly have been more appropriate, written and waiting for Nick Ryman, it seemed, generations before he had been conceived. 'See the Man who has Faith!' they had constantly called out – the very quality which had sustained the stationer turned wine-maker from Chorleywood.

'Would I have embarked upon the whole venture had I known what was in store?' Nick muses. 'Well, I have to answer by saying that because I am stupid, because I am pig-headed – call it what you like – that of course I would. I always say, "go for it". Otherwise the danger is that you turn round at the age of sixty and you say, "Why was I foolish enough not to at least have had a go?" The happy ending for me is that I have made peace with my son. And that hopefully one day he will come and live at Jaubertie. I have three lovely grandchildren. And it will be wonderful to see the place full of little people who will become larger, all laughing, just as the five of us did when we first came to Colombier.'

Nick likes to think of his bondholders as his extended family. Many of them over the years had written warm letters to him, while some had even visited him at the château. The memory of two standing ovations is still vivid and he looks with pride at the dinner service they gave him for his sixtieth birthday. It only remained for them to be informed of the changes which had taken place at the château in the Dordogne in which they too had had faith.

'Dear Bondholder,' he wrote. 'I started this "Club" in 1980 with 45 members. There are now over 380. I am 63 and have been working or playing soldier for the last 48 years and am ready to hand over to someone younger. I have been thinking about this for the last year, trying to find a person who is enthusiastic, qualified and who loves Jaubertie as much as I do. I have found him. He is my son, Hugh. I cannot tell you how happy I am.'